Understanding Key Education Issues

In this age of education innovation and reform, schools must evolve and react to current policy trends. This accessible book offers research-based insights into six key educational trends and issues that are impacting K-12 learning today: year-round schooling, assessments, educating minorities, anti-intellectualism, issues of social promotion and retention, and school design. Each chapter unpacks research and policy issues relating to these topics and provides administrators with practical advice on how they should approach these issues to improve learning in their schools. The ideas and strategies in *Understanding Key Education Issues* will help educators across the country achieve greater efficiency, better results, and a higher purpose.

Matthew Lynch is an award-winning writer, activist, and president of Lynch Consulting Group. Formerly, he was the Dean of the School of Education, Psychology, and Interdisciplinary Studies and an Associate Professor of Education at Virginia Union University, USA.

Other Eye on Education Books Available from Routledge
(www.routledge.com/eyeoneducation)

Ten Steps for Genuine Leadership in Schools
David M. Fultz

**College for Every Student:
A Practitioner's Guide to Building College and Career Readiness**
Rick Dalton and Edward P. St. John

Leading Learning for ELL Students: Strategies for Success
Catherine Beck and Heidi Pace

Leadership in America's Best Urban Schools
Joseph F. Johnson, Jr., Cynthia L. Uline, and Lynne G. Perez

The Power of Conversation: Transforming Principals into Great Leaders
Barbara Kohm

First Aid for Teacher Burnout: How You Can Find Peace and Success
Jenny G. Rankin

What Successful Principals Do! 199 Tips for Principals, 2nd Edition
Franzy Fleck

The Revitalized Tutoring Center: A Guide to Transforming School Culture
Jeremy Koselak and Brad Lyall

7 Ways to Transform the Lives of Wounded Students
Joe Hendershott

**School Leadership through the Seasons:
A Guide to Staying Focused and Getting Results All Year**
Ann T. Mausbach and Kimberly Morrison

**Distributed Leadership in Schools:
A Practical Guide for Learning and Improvement**
John A. DeFlaminis, Mustafa Abdul-Jabbar, and Eric Yoak

**The Leader's Guide to Working with Underperforming Teachers:
Overcoming Marginal Teaching and Getting Results**
by Sally Zepeda

Five Critical Leadership Practices: The Secret to High-Performing Schools
Ruth C. Ash and Pat H. Hodge

Understanding Key Education Issues

How We Got Here and Where We Go From Here

Matthew Lynch

Routledge
Taylor & Francis Group
NEW YORK AND LONDON

First published 2017
by Routledge
711 Third Avenue, New York, NY 10017

and by Routledge
2 Park Square, Milton Park, Abingdon, Oxon, OX14 4RN

Routledge is an imprint of the Taylor & Francis Group, an informa business

© 2017 Taylor & Francis

The right of Matthew Lynch to be identified as author of this work has been asserted by him in accordance with sections 77 and 78 of the Copyright, Designs and Patents Act 1988.

All rights reserved. No part of this book may be reprinted or reproduced or utilised in any form or by any electronic, mechanical, or other means, now known or hereafter invented, including photocopying and recording, or in any information storage or retrieval system, without permission in writing from the publishers.

Trademark notice: Product or corporate names may be trademarks or registered trademarks, and are used only for identification and explanation without intent to infringe.

Library of Congress Cataloging-in-Publication Data
Names: Lynch, Matthew, 1978–
Title: Understanding key education issues : how we got here and where we go from here / by Matthew Lynch.
Description: New York : Routledge, 2017. | Includes bibliographical references and index.
Identifiers: LCCN 2016048422 | ISBN 9781138285675 (hardback) | ISBN 9781138285682 (pbk.)
Subjects: LCSH: Education—United States.
Classification: LCC LA210 .L96 2017 | DDC 370.973—dc23
LC record available at https://lccn.loc.gov/2016048422

ISBN: 978-1-138-28567-5 (hbk)
ISBN: 978-1-138-28568-2 (pbk)
ISBN: 978-1-315-26881-1 (ebk)

Typeset in Optima
by Apex CoVantage, LLC

This book is dedicated to the teachers, administrators, parents, citizens, and politicians who have been fighting for genuine school reform in the United States for decades. Thank you for caring about our children.

This book is also dedicated to the children who were not properly educated by the US educational system. These children are the collateral damage that should spur us to create lasting change.

Contents

	Preface	viii
	Acknowledgments	xi
	Meet the Author	xii
1	How Did We Get Here, and What's Next?	1
2	Year-Round Schooling: The Unexpected Solution to America's Education Woes?	20
3	Examining the Present and Future of K-12 Assessments	41
4	Black Boys in Crisis: What Can We Do?	61
5	Combating Anti-Intellectualism and Academic Disengagement	83
6	Responding to Social Promotion and Retention	107
7	Rethinking School Design for Better Learning Outcomes	127

Preface

The formal education system was designed to meet the economic demands of the industrial revolution. However, in the current global economic climate, the established education system is struggling to meet the needs of a hyper-connected society that is in a constant state of evolution.

In this age of education innovation and reform, the pre-K through 12 classroom must evolve in order to adapt to the times. As a result, practices and policies are continually being reexamined and adjusted. The problem with many of these policy trends, however, is that they are strong on passionate discourse but weak on practical implementation and ideas. Furthermore, many are not based on evidence.

That is where this book comes in. It offers objective, research-based insights into six key educational trends and issues that are impacting the K-12 learning process: year-round schooling, assessments, educating minorities, anti-intellectualism, multiage classrooms, and the twin issues of social promotion and retention. At the same time, the book addresses controversial but important questions that relate to the future of public K-12 education in America. In addition, the book provides educators and administrators with practical strategies on how they should adjust to these new trends and issues, and how they can take advantage of them.

The first chapter looks at the history of the US education system. As America has grown in its nearly 250 years of existence, its public-school system has adjusted with the times. Various theories on properly educating our future generations have been introduced, tested, established, and then thrown out. Each new evolution of the public-school systems in the United States has built upon the lessons of the previous iteration, for better or for worse.

By identifying these historical trends and issues, we can start a journey that will lead us toward better outcomes for future generations. The premise of chapter one is that in order to understand where we are going and avoid the mistakes of the past, we first need to take a look at the history of education in America, focusing on past trends and issues. The chapter ends with an introduction of current trends and issues, which offers a perfect segue into chapter two.

The second chapter considers the current US school calendar, arguing that it is woefully outdated. It also makes suggestions on how the country can seamlessly transition into the more viable year-round calendar. The traditional school year, with roughly three months of vacation every summer, was first implemented when America was an agricultural society. Currently, over two million students in forty-six states attend school on year-round schedules. Based on current information, year-round schooling appears to offer an academic advantage to students. In particular, at-risk students fare better without a long summer break. I propose ways that the United States can transition fully to a year-round model and ditch the outdated traditional calendar for good. I also provide practical tips and strategies on how districts can seamlessly transition to a year-round schedule.

In chapter three, we look at standardized exams and other assessments. Many educators view standardized testing as a necessary evil of the improvement process. Proponents of standardized assessments say that without them, there is no adequate way to enforce educator accountability.

Assessments are a necessary part of education. This chapter outlines the steps needed to make K-12 assessments applicable to today's students, while discussing the assessment strategies that teachers and administrators need to use in order to positively impact academic achievement.

Chapter four looks at educating young black males in the United States. Study after study points to a crisis among African-American boys. The crisis begins in homes, is exacerbated by K-12 educational experiences, and often leads to a cycle of incarceration. What can be done to save this group of children that consistently seems to fall through the cracks? In this chapter, I look at the crisis among black males and provide educators with practical strategies for helping them succeed academically.

Chapter five looks at anti-intellectualism and academic disengagement in the American education system. All schools in the United States would claim to have an academic mission, but few seem interested in cultivating intellect. Every day 150 teens drop out of our schools and into poverty and prison. Too often, the culprit is a culture of anti-intellectualism. Chapter five looks at aspects of anti-intellectualism and provides teachers and administrators with strategies for confronting anti-intellectualism and academic disengagement in their school districts.

Chapter six considers how social promotion and retention are equally negative educational outcomes. Research shows that students who are held back, or who are socially promoted to the next grade, do not tend to do better in school and are at greater risk of dropping out. Students who experience these inappropriate grade-level shifts tend to be at higher risk of academic, social, and economic problems.

Chapter seven brings the book to a close by imagining what the necessary redesign of the American educational system might look like. This chapter delves into the idea of multiage and multi-ability classrooms, which loosen the strictures on children and teachers alike. Multiage classrooms have proven a resounding success where they have been tried. They tend to take care of the problems of social promotion and retention, and create a more stimulating learning environment. However, the shift to multiage classrooms requires an adjustment at all levels of the educational structure. The chapter looks at what those adjustments entail and at ways to simplify the redesign process.

The strategies in this book are deliberately designed to be workable in the educational system. If nothing else, I hope this book provides some discussion surrounding important questions that are often overlooked or under-considered in the current educational policy arena.

Acknowledgments

First, I would like to thank God for being my strength and my refuge. I would also like to acknowledge the collective unconscious of my ancestors. You paved the way for my ascendancy into the upper echelons of academia and served as a catalyst for my intellectual development.

Of course, I have to acknowledge my parents, Jessie and Patsy Lynch, for giving me their love and support. Also, I want to thank my sisters, Tammy Kemp and Angelina Lynch, for having my back. To their children, Adicuz, Kayla, Kerri, and Kelton: I hope my accomplishments will motivate each of you to live up to your limitless potential. No matter what, remember that your uncle loves you. You are the reason I am so passionate about reforming America's schools.

I would like to acknowledge my mentor, Dr. Rodney Washington, for his invaluable support, guidance, knowledge, and inspiration. Thanks for being the big brother that I never had! I also would like to acknowledge the invaluable support and guidance of my editor at Routledge, Heather Jarrow.

I also have to thank the scholars and academics who agreed to review this manuscript and provided invaluable feedback. Your assistance has ensured that my book is of the highest quality and will make a solid contribution to the K-12 educational arena.

Meet the Author

Dr. Matthew Lynch is an award-winning writer, activist, and president of Lynch Consulting Group. Formerly, he was the Dean of the School of Education, Psychology, and Interdisciplinary Studies and an Associate Professor of Education at Virginia Union University. Prior to his career in higher education, he spent seven years as a K-12 teacher—an experience that gave him an intimate view of the challenges facing genuine education reform.

Dr. Lynch has focused the second stage of his career on researching topics related to educational reform, the achievement gap, and teacher education. He believes that improving teacher education is an essential component in closing the achievement gap.

Meet the Author

Dr. Lynch's articles and op-eds appear regularly in the *Huffington Post*, *Diverse: Issues in Higher Education*, and *Education Week*. He has written numerous peer-reviewed articles, which have appeared in academic journals such as the *AASA Journal of Scholarship and Practice*, *International Journal of Progressive Education*, and *Academic Leadership Journal*. In addition, he has authored and edited a number of books on school reform and school leadership. These include *It's Time for a Change* (Rowman & Littlefield, 2011), *A Guide to Effective School Leadership Theories* (Routledge, 2012), *Before Obama: A Reappraisal of Black Reconstruction Era Politicians* (Praeger, 2012), and *The Call to Teach* (Pearson, 2014).

Please visit his website at www.drmattlynch.com for more information.

How Did We Get Here, and What's Next?

- The state of the American school system: What do our schools look like to an outside observer?
- The birth of the American public school: The European origins of our school system and the one-room schoolhouse.
- The Mann reforms to public education: Horace Mann's nineteenth-century advancements, which continue to influence educational policy.
- Public education as national requirement: The first public schools and how they operated.
- Unified, then divided, public schools: Unity following the World Wars soon dissolved.
- A nation of public-school students at risk: The realization that America was no longer on top of the world, and the attempts to rectify that.
- Minority education in America: A look at the horrific legacy of disenfranchised students, which continues to the present day.
- A melting pot of educational ideology: A look at the present cacophony of ideas and programs, and a glance toward the future.

Innovation has always driven Americans and continues to be a driving force today. It's what has simultaneously given us the labels of "crazy" and "genius," and is what makes Americans a global power to be reckoned with. The Wright brothers, Thomas Edison, George Washington Carver, Henry Ford, Steve Jobs . . . the list of world-changing thinkers and inventors is long. Without the many Americans who have stepped outside the lines to better their own ways of life and those of their fellow citizens, this nation would not be considered the greatest on the globe.

That creative spirit is born in our public schools. The students who will dream up tomorrow's major inventions and come up with plans to improve the American way of life and fill every job in between are in our K-12 classrooms today. In spite of all their problems, public schools remain a steadfast reminder of all that is great and inspirational about the American way.

As America has grown in its nearly 250 years of existence, its public-school system has adjusted with the times (Urban and Wagoner 2009). Various theories on properly educating our future generations have been introduced, tested, established, and then thrown out. Each new evolution of the public-school systems in the United States—from the one-room schoolhouse to compulsory education to opening the doors of education for all citizens—has built upon the lessons of the ones before (both good and bad).

The State of the American School System

What do our school systems look like from an objective perspective? If you base your knowledge of the nation's public schools on news headlines alone, you might have a bleak perception of what is happening in the K-12 classrooms funded by our tax dollars. A report issued by the US Department of Education in April of 2014 showed that high school seniors did not show any signs of improvement in math and science scores from 2009 to 2013 (Nation's Report Card 2014). When compared with other developed countries, US students lag seriously behind in areas such as math and science, too. The students who are bringing down the national averages are not just from underprivileged areas. A *Washington Examiner* report found that more than half of fifteen-year-olds from homes with well-educated parents are not proficient in at least one of the three key subject areas: reading, math, and science (Peterson 2014).

Despite these and numerous similar reports, US high school seniors are graduating at a record rate of 80 percent (Hefling 2014). This is a statistic that should no doubt be celebrated, but it does raise a question mark: How are so many US students lagging behind in so many vital academic areas, yet graduating from our schools at record rates?

The truth is complicated. Standards for exactly what students should be learning at every step of their educational journey have never been more stringent. The *No Child Left Behind* (NCLB) legislation enacted in

2001 heightened educator accountability systems and put stricter assessment processes in place to measure the true learning outcomes of students (Klein 2015). Teacher accountability was in place before NCLB, and so were state assessment tests, but the legislation placed both on a pedestal that many schools are still unable to attain. By setting blanket benchmarks for the entire nation, based on limited testing materials, teachers were essentially stripped of their free will when it came to educating and were forced to begin "teaching to the test." For many educators, NCLB marked an end to learning for learning's sake in classrooms. For some, it meant dumbing down materials to ensure all students scored well on those vital assessments.

Fast forward twelve years to the recent enactment of the Common Core Standards in forty-four states and the District of Columbia, and accountability and assessments have even more to contend with. Tied to President Obama's federal funding program Race to the Top, Common Core benchmarks were determined by the National Governors Association. States could choose to opt in or out, with pressure to conform enhanced by the promise of plentiful funds. Like NCLB legislation (which still exists alongside Common Core requirements), the new set of initiatives seeks stronger student outcomes in areas such as math, science, and technology (Core Standards 2016).

In theory, Common Core Standards should work: Place more focus on the subjects where American students need extra help, attach some money as an incentive, and then watch the test scores rise. The true effectiveness of these standards remains to be seen, but it is hard to imagine that placing greater concentration on a narrower range of subjects will end up assisting this generation of K-12 students (Mathis 2010).

Assessments and teacher accountability tethered to funding are just the tip of the iceberg when it comes to the issues holding back the actual process of learning in our public schools. Overcrowding and inequality of resources, as well as a cultural shift toward anti-intellectualism, weigh heavily on the schools within our borders.

By identifying the major trends and issues that hinder the effectiveness of the public schools of our nation, we can start a journey that will lead us toward better outcomes for future generations. It is not a task reserved for educators alone, however. To bring about the necessary changes, it will take the involvement every parent, business owner, and community member. But in order to understand where we are going and avoid the mistakes of the past, we first need to take a look at the history of education in America, focusing on the anti-intellectual trends.

The Birth of the American Public School

There were public schools in America as far back as the mid-1600s, in the Massachusetts Bay Colony, but the precursors of the modern public school began appearing in Pennsylvania at the end of the eighteenth century. Even the poorest of citizens was welcomed through those schoolhouse doors and offered a public education. (Note, however, that African Americans and Native Americans were not considered citizens at that time.) The New York Public School Society was established in 1805, and by 1870 all states had at least a minimal public program in place to educate students en masse. These programs were mostly voluntary, however—compulsory education would not become widespread until the beginning of the twentieth century (Urban and Wagoner 2009).

What was taught in these early schools varied by region but was grounded in a basic set of rules. Public education was meant to unite American families through a common interest: raising educated children who would soon be at the helm of the nation's future. Basic education was not something reserved for the elite. Reading, writing, and basic arithmetic were necessities of living as Americans and were important when it came to guiding the young nation (Urban and Wagoner 2009).

The learning resources of early America were understandably limited. There was not much variety in American-made textbooks or other learning tools. Much of what was used in these schools were texts developed in England and repurposed for American pursuits. Educators recognized the need for purely American educational texts, though, and slowly they began to take shape (Urban and Wagoner 2009).

In the 1780s, Noah Webster set out to create a textbook that would teach children the realities of spelling in the new land. Until that point, spelling textbooks were primarily imports from England that sought to teach kids the most unusual and difficult, yet least used, words in the English language. Webster saw the impracticality of this and set out to change it. *The American Spelling Book* became a staple for learning in homes and in the few organized educational schoolrooms that existed. In accomplishing this, Webster established the first systematic method for learning in the young country. It was practical, easy to navigate, and widely used. As late as 1866, after many other spelling books had been written and updated, Webster's original version was still selling nine million copies annually (Svobdny 1985; Webster 1783).

From the outset, public education in the United States was about moving students collectively in the direction the nation wanted to go. Individualism and customized learning were certainly not common terms, and the choices for education were slim. The accepted curriculum for one American was deemed good enough for another. This base learning was rooted in the need to not only obtain knowledge, but to use education as a way to build up a nation that was still teetering dangerously on the edge of failure. Parents did not encourage their children to learn spelling or arithmetic so they could have a better life, but so they could continue to have a free one. Education was a means of survival, and banding together with the same education goals, at least when it came to common people, was a way to build the entire nation up. Certainly there was some educational elitism through private schooling and university systems, but when it came to the public institutions of learning, every student encountered the same knowledge set (Unger 2007).

As the country continued to expand, both in population and land mass, public education became more segmented. Until the 1840s, public schools were under local control, with little input from the state and virtually no federal oversight. Attendance was rising, however. The US Census from 1840 shows that 3.68 million children from ages five to fifteen attended school, representing about 55 percent of the population in that age bracket. Around this time the idea of one-room schoolhouses took shape, with the older students acting as helpers for the younger ones. There was no formal credentialing for teachers. This was why young single women often filled the roles: Unlike young men, who were toiling on the farms, young women were available, so they served as teachers until they got married (Unger 2007).

The Mann Reforms to Public Education

The first attempt at regulating exactly what American students were learning in those early schoolhouses came in 1837 from education reformer Horace Mann. When he took over the role of Secretary of Education in

Massachusetts, he set out to create a common way of teaching educational content, particularly to elementary students. For the most part, he adapted his ideas from a Prussian model that stressed training for educators (Messerli 1972).

Along with shared content, Mann's reforms brought about the first age-grade systems where students were promoted based on age, not academic aptitude. While this led to greater concentration on subjects that increased in difficulty as students grew older, it also planted the notion that American students should be passive learners, as opposed to active ones. The idea that each student should master by a certain time content based on broadly accepted criteria was established as a way to keep students moving through the public-education system (Messerli 1972).

States rushed to duplicate Mann's ideas in their own schools and multiage classrooms disappeared in the coming decades. As the American population rose, it made sense to accommodate students in a more segmented way. Age-grading was meant to improve efficiency of classrooms and the entire public-education system. The more students who could be passed through the public schools, the better. It made economic sense and, in the minds of reformers such as Mann, it would lead to a more highly educated public (Messerli 1972).

Though Mann's system for age grading was introduced over 175 years ago, it remains the primary form of organization in American schools today. While some students are retained (or held back) when they do not master the material at hand, the idea of socially promoting students based solely on their ages is more popular than one might think. It is difficult to measure exactly how many students are passed on to the next grade based more on age than academic merit, because teachers are obviously not keen to admit it. Retaining students is simple to measure but only tells half the story. Of the students who are not retained, how many of them should be? (Messerli 1972).

Sending children to school later throws a wrench in the traditional age-grade system. Teachers are often ill prepared to deal with students who are outside the age specifications in their classrooms, and in cases where both a five- and seven-year-old are in the same classroom, there are naturally differences in behavior and maturity. By adhering strictly to an age-grade system for just some, it puts a strain on the others. Teachers who hope to avoid problems for their colleagues in higher grades often take the easier route of age-grading promotion.

Despite the pitfalls engendered by the age-grading system, the positive impact of Mann's endeavors should not go unnoticed. Along with age-grading, he emphasized the need for mandatory attendance. Mann insisted that public education was not a perk of American life; it was a necessity for the well-being of our nation. He believed that for the nation to truly advance, its youth belonged in classrooms, not just in fields or factories, and that states should implement attendance policies to support this view. While it took some time for his ideas to see mass adoption, his advocacy for mandatory public schools found some resonance. By 1900, thirty-four states had implemented required-schooling laws, thirty of which required students to stay in school until the age of fourteen. Ten years later, 72 percent of the children in the United States went to school. Just a decade after that, every state had required attendance policies. By 1940, half of all young adults in the United States were high school diploma recipients (Wells 1975).

Public Education as National Requirement

By the early 1900s, the idea that every American child had the right to an education had gained mass adoption. Even students destined for a life in the mines or on the railroads deserved basic spelling, arithmetic, and science lessons. Public schools were a place to absorb the common learning priorities that other students were also absorbing throughout the country. This view of public schools gave all (white) children an equitable start in life, at least when it came to actual curriculum presented. From there, the students were free to carve out the lives they wanted, or follow a predetermined path based on family or geographic limitations (Unger 2007).

Just after the start of the twentieth century, a new public-education ideology began to emerge that hinted that schools should be utilized as more than places to memorize facts. According to reformers such as University of Chicago professor John Dewey, public schools needed to serve a greater good—for the individual and the country. Dewey was a figurehead of the Progressive Movement, which insisted schools be socially conscious places where more than book learning took place. While Dewey's theories were widely discussed, they did not see blanket adoption at the height of his popularity. Much like the public-school districts of today, Dewey faced red tape at every turn and an entrenched antipathy toward change ("John Dewey" n.d.). In the eyes of education bureaucrats, schools were established for learning what was written in a textbook, not for stimulating students to think about social issues.

Though slow to gain adoption in his own time, Dewey's notion of public schools as agents for socialization and change for the better is certainly evident in school systems today. Consider public awareness campaigns, like First Lady Nancy Reagan's "Just Say No" initiative, which infiltrated schools in the 1980s, or the emphasis on Earth Day every April in public schools throughout the nation, or First Lady Michelle Obama's "Let's Move" campaign, which offers health-awareness programs to schools.

Along with the basic knowledge that accompanies the facts in textbooks, K-12 students in America are expected to acquire a set of life truths before they graduate, such as that smoking and drugs will kill you, and stealing is bad. Though not religious institutions, public schools have transformed in the past century from agents of factual information to ethics delivery centers. It is not enough for students to pass a test at the end of each grade and at the end of a K-12 career; to be true contributors to society, they must have moral compasses and understand the responsibilities of citizenship.

Though his theories were not particularly political, Dewey's ethically minded approach fed into the nation's thirst for patriotism. Part of contributing to society was having an appreciation for society and its symbolism. Consider the morning ritual of every public school in the nation since the early 1920s: reciting the Pledge of Allegiance (Biography n.d.).

Unified, then Divided, Public Schools

Public education in the United States remained primarily unchanged throughout the First and Second World Wars. Improvements in communication, particularly through radio transmissions, offered schools a window into the worldwide battles. Though not part of any textbook or measured testing, wartime knowledge was prized in public schools and patriotism swelled. Unlike the Civil War, which divided the nation, the World Wars in the first half of the twentieth century knit the union more tightly together. As millions of men fought outside US soil, women filled historically male job roles and children continued to attend school. Going to school and learning became a sign of solidarity with the soldiers on the frontlines (Spring 2009).

However, the sense of unity in public education was all but destroyed in the 1950s and 1960s as issues of desegregation plagued the nation. Most Americans celebrated the changes, of course, but enough citizens opposed desegregation that it was a bleak time in US public-school history. If public education was, after all, meant to provide common knowledge and life skills in equal ways to all children in America, then the theory of "separate but equal" certainly needed to be deposed. Change is difficult, though, even in one of the most progressive nations in the world. The solidarity in public-school classrooms faded and was replaced with controversy. These two decades mark an important shift in the role and perception of public schools in America. Before schools started taking on bigger issues like desegregation, abuse, and childhood hunger, they were places that served the needs of the nation. That tide turned in the mid-1900s, as public schools began to lead instead of follow. Public schools stopped adhering to what was dictated for its next generation in terms of learning and citizenship and began to blaze a trail for the rest of society where collective belief systems were concerned. It may have been too late to change the minds of disenfranchised adults who had grown up accepting their worlds in a particular way, but it was still possible to change the minds of students (Spring 2009).

Schools became the vehicles for future change, starting with the youth of the nation. The focus was no longer just on economics or raising ideal citizens; core ideologies were being shaped in public-school classrooms across the nation.

This characteristic of public schools is still evident today. Take anti-bullying campaigns, for example—particularly as they relate to lesbian, gay, bisexual, and transgender students. While many parents (and even some school boards) are fighting against anti-bullying policies that are designed to protect LGBT students, schools across the country are adopting them at a rapid pace. The same is true of healthy eating programs and the push to get kids away from television and computers and involved in active pursuits. Schools cannot change what is being taught at home, or even what students themselves believe. However, by implementing change through example and policy, the hope is that future generations will have a different take on important issues than their parents did. Like the efforts of Dewey, public schools try to establish principles that will then influence a particular group of K-12 students as adults (Spring 2009).

The 1970s brought even more equality to public schools with the passage of the Education for All Handicapped Children Act. This was the first federal regulation mandating that public schools accepting federal funding also provide a free education and meals to children with mental or physical disabilities. It was not enough to simply accept the students; schools had to create a teaching plan that would give these students as close to a typical education as their non-handicapped peers as possible. Though separate classrooms were inherent to the plan, schools were instructed to keep special-education students in as close physical proximity to their peers as possible. Public schools thus became even stronger when it came to truly opening their doors for all students and being a right of American life (Spring 2009).

A Nation of Public-School Students at Risk

During the 1980s, American educators and the public first became concerned in a sweeping way about the quality of education in tax-funded schools. In 1981, the National Commission on Excellence in Education was formed. The group released *A Nation at Risk*, an in-depth report that warned against the dangers that could result from mediocrity in US public schools. Though the concern should have been purely based on the learning aspect of American students, there were larger worries that loomed, primarily concerning the nation's economic future. It marked the first time in the history of public schools in America that citizens began to compare students to those in other developed countries such as Japan, China, and even England. The assumption that America the Beautiful was also the best at everything, including educating children, was shaken. People started to worry about where the youth of the nation would guide them in coming years (National Commission on Excellence in Education 1983).

Reforms started to take place, but at the local level. Schools took it upon themselves to correct the problem of incompetent and uncaring students by adding graduation requirements and raising teacher salaries. Universities jumped in by heightening the requirements for young educators to earn their degrees in an attempt to give K-12 students an advantage through the resource of stronger teachers. Free-response and short-essay options were beginning to gain favor with educators across the country as indicators of what students had really comprehended. Multiple-choice options started to fade from routine school exams, though we should note that they are still the primary way state assessments are delivered today. As a matter of efficiency, these easily scanned answer sheets make the most sense. As a way to truly assess what students do and do not know, however, they are lacking (Spring 2009).

The drive for higher quality education carried over into the 1990s, but instead of a renewed dedication to the goals of public education, the American public and reformers looked outside for answers. The phrase "school choice" began to resonate throughout the country, with people wondering what could be done to funnel public dollars to alternatives to public schools. Funding for religiously aligned schools had been discussed over a hundred years earlier, when it was first suggested that parochial schools receive a government stipend to help with expenses. Fearing the rising Irish Catholic population, state lawmakers put the kibosh on any such plans, citing separation of church and state. As parents began to question the value of the public-school education provided to their kids, they began to feel entitled to different choices when the tax-funded school in their area performed under par (Spring 2009).

A new ideology began to take shape in the form of charter schools—publicly funded non-religious schools that were given the freedom to innovate outside the constraints of public-school regulations. To some, it seemed like a smart way to provide more educational options while lighting a fire under public schools, which until then had faced no real competition. To critics, the plan to use taxpayer dollars to fund new schools only directed the money away from the place where it was really needed: actual public schools. The school-choice debate still rages today, with a renewed call for vouchers for religious schools thrown into the mix (Spring 2009).

The 1990s also ushered in a new age of accountability in public schools, triggered by the quality concerns raised in the 1980s. The roots of the 2002 *No Child Left Behind Act* were planted in 1990s educational reform movements. NCLB was a reenactment of the outdated Elementary and Secondary Education Act of 1965. Both acts focused on ways to bring higher levels of equality to public education, but NCLB also had a strong focus on bolstering student test scores and ensuring teachers were liable. NCLB put new pressures to heighten achievement on every educator, from top education policymakers to teachers in the classroom (Klein 2015).

While NCLB has been under fire almost from its genesis, the truth is that it remained a large part of the educational system in America's public-school classrooms until 2015. The release and adoption of Common Core Standards in 2013 took the ideology of NCLB to a new level. Though their adoption is voluntary, these new accountability measures seem eerily similar to the federally mandated ones of NCLB. Instead of getting away from empty assessments that often take the shape of multiple-choice questions, it seems that public-school systems are simply adding to the void. It's not a pretty picture, but it is the reality of what educators are facing right now, and it will certainly impact this generation of K-12 students (Klein 2015).

At the end of December 2015, President Obama signed the Every Student Succeeds Act (ESSA) into law, effectively sweeping away NCLB (Nelson 2015). The new bill made major changes to federal education policy. One thing that changed with the ESSA was how teacher performance is evaluated. States now have the ability to individually appraise how well its teachers are doing performance-wise. Another alteration under the new law will allow states "to come up with their own way to determine the quality of their local schools." This means that test scores are no longer the sole deciding factor for school performance.

ESSA lists music as a component of a well-rounded education and gives it more support than previous policies when it comes to access and funding. The law also means federal grant funding is opened for states and local school districts to support music education programs and further train music teachers. ESSA has been a long time coming. Considering that NCLB had needed an update since 2007, it is shocking how long it took to sign this new law.

Minority Education in America

The recounting of education to this point has been just one side of the American story. There are, of course, many parallel versions of how the youth of America have been educated since the founding of the nation. Perhaps the most impactful is the history of how black children, before and after Abolition, have fit into the educational system.

In the early days of the nation, there were no public-school options available to black children. Even states that outlawed slavery did not offer public education to residents who were of color. In Southern states deeply entrenched in slave culture, the education of black children was actually illegal. White slave owners believed that literacy and knowledge would threaten the slave system and so laws were passed to forbid it. For example, in South Carolina a sum of one hundred pounds was demanded of anyone caught teaching a slave to read or write (PBS n.d.).

Slavery laws aside, the first fifty years following the signing of the Constitution were not focused on education for children of any race. For black children, there were some limited educational options in the form of religious schools. The exact intent of these schools was likely more about conversion than bringing equality to black Americans through education, but the learning scenarios did exist. The French Catholics in Louisiana had established schools for black students as early as the 1600s, and the Pennsylvania Quakers would follow suit in the 1700s (Questia 2014). The first African Free School opened in New York City in 1787 with the express mission of educating black children in order to bring them educational equality with their white peers (Dubois and Provenzo 2002). Like other schools of the time period, the African Free Schools began as one-room schoolhouses. Public funds were first funneled to these schools in 1824—an extreme departure at the time (Spring 2009).

Public schools for slaves and free black children in larger numbers began to pop up in the nineteenth century. Maine was the first state to grant public-school privileges to students of all races in 1820, and Rhode Island voted to do the same in 1843. Black teachers at public schools made less than their white counterparts—with the exception of Washington, DC, where teachers were considered federal employees and were paid the same regardless of where they taught (Spring 2009).

In 1849, a young African-American girl, Sarah C. Roberts, was refused entrance to the public school that was closest to her home "on the sole ground of color." Her father, Benjamin F. Roberts, was told by the authorities that he would have to enroll his daughter in one of the two public schools in Boston that catered to black students. Both schools were a considerable distance from his home, and getting his daughter to and from school would have dramatically inconvenienced his family. Roberts tried in two successive years to enroll little Sarah in the nearby school. When he was rejected for the second time he brought a lawsuit against the city, citing a Massachusetts statute stating that any person who was excluded from attaining a public-school education could recover damages from the city. Though Roberts's lawsuit eventually failed, it generated enormous public interest and considerable sympathy for the plight of African-American students. Seven years later, largely as a knock-on effect of the Roberts case, the Massachusetts legislature changed the state policy to make it illegal to refuse any public-school student based on race. The case was to influence the Supreme Court when, three-quarters of a century later, it would look at segregation in schools in the famous *Brown v. Board of Education* case (Kull 1992).

Even when public schools opened their doors to black students, they were separated from their white peers, thus establishing the practice of segregation in America's public schools. Following the Civil War, states were required to provide public education to black students, thus ushering in the establishment of Jim Crow laws pertaining to education. These practices followed the law when it came to providing a public education to black Americans, but kept black students separate from white ones. The phrase "separate but equal" was offered as justification for the segregation, but public schools were far from equitable (Spring 2009).

Schools for black children throughout the country lacked resources and overcrowding flourished despite there being many less black children in school than white ones. As far back as 1900, black schools in Virginia had 37 percent more students per school building than white ones and, in the late 1930s, black school properties were valued at only one-third of white ones (Virginia Historical Society n.d.).

Despite all the strides public education has made in equality in the past 150 years, schools with majority black populations still tend to be the most overcrowded and underfunded. In the summer of 2013, the Chicago Board of Education voted to close fifty public schools in the city. Of the students impacted by the school closures, 88 percent were black and 94 percent came from low-income households (Kilkenny 2013). Those students were then sent to other schools, further crowding them. During the school year ending in 2011, there were 670 New York City schools with student-to-teacher ratios above accepted contract levels—the majority of which served minority students (Kuczynski-Brown 2012). Despite the guise of public, equitable schools, overcrowding remains a very significant problem when it comes to the nation's black and disadvantaged students.

The results of limited black public and private primary education in the nineteenth century were the first African-American college graduates. Following the end of the Civil War, the first "black" colleges were established and, by 1900, more than two thousand African-American students had earned college degrees. However, despite a dramatic rise in that number over the next century, it was not until 1985 that Harvard University appointed its first black tenured professor (Fitzgerald 2011).

Black students are not the only ones who have faced disadvantages when navigating the US educational system. While K-12 students today may imagine that the *Brown v. Board of Education* ruling in 1954 marked the end of injustice in America's public schools, the journey toward true equality in education has still been laborious. Sixty years later, it remains a work in progress (Dubois and Provenzo 2002).

There is still an achievement gap between white students on the one hand and black and other minority students on the other. The National Assessment of Educational Progress consistently finds large achievement gaps, or lags in academic success, between one student demographic and another—between white and minority students. The latest comprehensive data, from 2009, indicate that there is a 26 percent gap in achievement in both mathematics and reading between fourth- and eighth-grade Hispanic students and their white peers. For black students, the numbers were similar. Reading scores saw an achievement gap of 27 percent for fourth graders and 26 percent for eighth graders. In math, black students had an achievement gap disadvantage of 26 percent for fourth graders and 31 percent for eighth graders (National Assessment of Education Progress 2013).

Since laws are in place to prevent inequality from infringing on K-12 education, why aren't they working? Is there some unspoken prejudice against minority groups that is keeping each generation of K-12 students from achieving as much as their white peers? Though there are certainly plenty of conspiracy theories out there, the truth is much more complex.

Minorities have always had a tough time in America, in education and otherwise. Think back to the large Irish immigration of the late nineteenth century. This group of people in search of basic needs such as food, shelter, and religious freedom faced an uphill battle when they arrived on US soil. The prevalence of the Catholic school system today is due in part to the need for the institutions when Irish children were refused an education, or were severely bullied and discriminated against in public or other private settings. Generally speaking, first-generation immigrants and their children have less, live in poorer neighborhoods, and struggle on a greater scale with assimilation and language barriers. This is nothing new, but it does impact the contemporary students in today's classrooms.

The Hispanic population in the United States, for example, grew 43 percent from the 2000 to 2010 Census reports, accounting for more than half of the total US population increase. These students are already at a disadvantage to their peers who were born and raised on US soil because of language, social, and cultural barriers. And yes, there is some outright prejudice and discrimination too. The difference between these first-generation American students and those from a century ago is that fanning the flames of underachievement and intolerance is no longer acceptable—which gives them an advantage over their immigrant predecessors and leaves at least a glimmer of light that achievement gaps can be narrowed or eliminated.

Differences in achievement of minorities are also based on simple logistics. In most states, public-school selection is based on location—making true integration of the races impossible. Most black students are still segregated in to schools in predominantly black neighborhoods, and Hispanic students tend to gravitate toward inner-city and urban schools that deal with larger issues of overcrowding and underfunding. If minorities attend majority-white schools, they seldom feel comfortable in their surroundings. The basic public-school principle of schooling students in their own neighborhoods or districts, which seems logical on the surface, has actually led to segregation and unfair educational opportunities.

Some of the barriers thrown up by districting are starting to come down. This is due to states such as California and New Jersey allowing for intra- and inter-district options for students. The implementation of public charter and magnet schools, or privately run schools that use state funding and are tuition-free, have also given black students more options when it comes to choosing their schools, instead of being confined to the ones in their neighborhoods. However, the jury is still out on whether these tactics actually help or hinder the minority community as a whole. Does fleeing public schools, and trying desperately to escape disadvantaged neighborhoods, enhance or undercut these communities?

A Melting Pot of Educational Ideology

Looking at the public-school systems of today, there seems to be a marked return to the roots of the US education system in the late 1700s. Students are once again being corralled into career paths and being prescribed the best course to reach workforce goals in the fastest way possible. Children as young as five are being enrolled in specialty schools for math, science, or the performing arts and quarantined from their peers on other specific or general paths. It has become the job of parents and teachers to discover for their students exactly what they should do with their working lives a full twelve years before those careers start. The general feeling seems to be: if schools aren't prepping their students to ace assessments, get into colleges, and end up in the perfect career that fits their talents, then what good are they?

This teach-to-career mentality has infiltrated even the highest ranks of American society. President Obama's Race to the Top program links federal funding to states, following a point system that relies heavily on assessment of the materials deemed most important for US students to be learning—much of which is determined by the increasing need for math, science, technology, and engineering occupations in the United States (White House, "Race to the Top" n.d.).

President Obama has also been vocal about his support for stronger technology programs to meet the expected explosion of computer science and related job fields in the next half decade. His "Educate to Innovate" campaign is designed to move US students from the middle to the top of science and math achievement in the next decade. This initiative relies on interactive games, private partnerships with organizations such as the Bill and Melinda Gates Foundation, and national science competitions, with visits to the White House as prizes ("Educate to Innovate" n.d.).

However, despite the strides Americans have made since post-Revolutionary days, we seem to have the same archaic mindset when it comes to our schools—specifically those that are publicly funded. Education is inextricably tied to our perception of what it will earn individual students and the economy as a whole, and not to the pursuit and furthering of learning as a nation.

Do public schools prepare all students adequately for the college and the workforce? Not by a long shot. There is still a lot that is right about our public schools, though. In a world that often seems fraught with inequality and discrimination, public schools can be equalizers. They don't always provide the same quality of education to students of differing socioeconomic backgrounds, but the principles are there. Public schools do serve as the main agent of positive change between one generation and the next, however, and bring the right of an education to students exactly where they are.

References

Biography. n.d. "John Dewey." Accessed September 9, 2016. http://www.biography.com/people/john-dewey-9273497.

Core Standards. "About the Standards." Accessed September 9, 2016. http://www.corestandards.org/about-the-standards/.

Dubois, W.E.B., and E. F. Provenzo. 2002. *Du Bois on Education*. Lanham, MD: Rowman & Littlefield.

Fitzgerald, Jim. 2011. "1st Tenured Black Professor at Harvard Law Dies." *Yahoo! News*. Accessed September 9, 2016. https://www.yahoo.com/news/1st-tenured-black-professor-harvard-law-dies-194952120.html.

Hefling, Kimberly. 2014. "Report: 4 in 5 U.S. High School Students Graduate." *The Associated Press*, 4(28), 1.

Kilkenny, Allison. 2013. "Teachers, Parents Complain Overcrowding, Lack of Support Plague 'Welcoming Schools'." *The Nation*, 12(9), 2. Accessed June 3, 2014. http://www.thenation.com/blog/177515/teachers-parents-complain-overcrowding-lack-support-plague-welcoming-schools#.

Klein, Alyson. 2015. "No Child Left Behind: An Overview." *Education Week*, April 10. Accessed September 9, 2016. http://www.edweek.org/ew/section/multimedia/no-child-left-behind-overview-definition-summary.html.

Kuczynski-Brown, Alex. 2012. "New York Class Size: Nearly Half of Public Schools Have Overcrowded Classrooms, UFT Says." *The Huffington Post*, September 26, 2012. Accessed September 9, 2016. http://www.huffingtonpost.com/2012/09/26/new-york-class-size-uft_n_1914357.html.

Kull, A. 1992. *The Color-Blind Constitution*. Cambridge, MA: Harvard University Press.

Mathis, W. J. 2010. *The "Common Core" Standards Initiative: An Effective Reform Tool?* Boulder and Tempe: Education and the Public Interest Center & Education Policy Research Unit.

Messerli, J. 1972. *Horace Mann: A Biography*. New York: Random House.

National Assessment of Education Progress. 2013. "Achievement Gaps." Accessed June 8, 2014. http://nces.ed.gov/nationsreportcard/studies/gaps/.

The National Commission on Excellence in Education. 1983. *A Nation at Risk: The Imperative for Educational Reform*. Arlington, VI: Eric Document Reproduction Service.

Nation's Report Card. 2014. Accessed September 9, 2016. http://www.nationsreportcard.gov/#/.

Nelson, Libby. 2015. "How Schools Will Be Different Without No Child Left Behind." *Vox*. Accessed September 9, 2016. http://www.vox.com/2015/12/11/9889350/every-student-succeeds-act-schools.

PBS. n.d. "Africans in America." Accessed June 3, 2014. http://www.pbs.org/wgbh/aia/part4/4h2945.html.

Peterson, Paul E. 2014. "Study Finds U.S. Students Lag Behind Those in Other Industrialized Countries." *Washington Examiner*, 5(13), 1.

Questia. 2014. "History of African-American Education." Accessed June 2, 2014. http://www.questia.com/library/education/education-in-different-countries-and-states/history-of-african-american-education.

Spring, J. 2009. *American Education*. 14th edition. New York: McGraw-Hill.

Svobdny, Dolly. 1985. *Early American Textbooks, 1775–1900*. Washington, DC: U.S. Department of Education.

Unger, H. G. 2007. *Encyclopedia of American Education*. 3rd edition. New York: Facts on File.

Urban, W. J., and J. L. Wagoner. 2009. *American Education: A History*. New York: Routledge.

The Virginia Historical Society. n.d. "Beginnings of Black Education." Accessed June 3, 2013. http://www.vahistorical.org/collections-and-resources/virginia-history-explorer/civil-rights-movement-virginia/beginnings-black?legacy=true.

Webster, N. 1783. *The American Spelling Book*. Self-published.

Wells, Elizabeth M. 1975. *Divine Songs by Isaac Watts*. Fairfax, VA: Thoburn Press.

White House. n.d. "Educate to Innovate." Accessed September 9, 2016. https://www.whitehouse.gov/issues/education/k-12/educate-innovate.

White House. n.d. "Race to the Top." Accessed September 9, 2016. https://www.whitehouse.gov/issues/education/k-12/race-to-the-top.

Year-Round Schooling
The Unexpected Solution to America's Education Woes?

- Do it for the kids—especially those at risk: Year-round schooling would help minority students and lessen the summer slide.
- But won't this stress out the teachers? There are no summers off and more red tape. However, these issues are outweighed by the advantages.
- The issue of pay: How does year-round schooling affect teacher salaries?
- Can year-round schooling save the economy? There are on-campus costs and savings, as well as community cost and savings involved in year-round schooling.
- Adding more days to the school year: Are all the school days considered equal?
- The pitfalls of changing the status quo: Addressing the issues of rising costs, lack of enough downtime, and scheduling adjustments.
- How to implement a year-round schooling system in your school district: Choosing an implementation team and steps toward implementation.
- Operational strategies for special services: Special day classes and how to evaluate in a year-round schooling system.

The United States is known for a lot of things, but a superior educational system is not one of them. Throughout most of America, schools have summers off. Could this be one reason the K-12 educational system is struggling to keep students engaged? Year-round schooling offers a promising solution to our educational system's problems. Here's a breakdown of the effects year-round schooling has on students, teachers, and even the economy.

When public schools first started cropping up in the United States, they were considered secondary to other hands-on pursuits. Learning to read, write, and perform basic arithmetic in classrooms was considered less respectable than the physical labor of building the nation and keeping up family farms.

Even when a basic public-school education became a priority, the school calendar revolved around agriculture—a necessity of the American way of life. Three months off in the summer months was not mandated because students needed downtime, free creative play, or time to decompress after their strenuous studies. Those months off were full of even more work, for the sake of the family and the nation.

Though family farms have for the most part become an antiquated piece of American history, the idea of summers off from school remains alive and well. The American Enterprise Institute for Public Policy Research finds that the average American student receives thirteen weeks off of school each calendar year—with ten or eleven of those coming consecutively during June, July, and August. Few other countries have more than seven weeks off in a school calendar. Around 10 percent of US schools have transitioned to a year-round school calendar, with shorter breaks inserted throughout the year, but the majority of schools in the United States still follow a summers-off schedule (Morin 2016).

Why do we persist with an antiquated system? There is no longer an economic reason for summer vacation, and there is no medical reason that three consecutive months during the center of the calendar year are necessary for the healthy development of children. The reason the school year remains in a summers-off state is simple: it is easier than changing it. That mentality begins with teachers in the classroom and escalates to educational policymakers. Changing the ways things have always been, even if there is some pretty solid evidence that it would improve things, is too cumbersome—so why bother?

Do It for the Kids—Especially Those at Risk

It Would Help Minority Students

Anna Habash of Education Trust, a nonprofit that works with schools to better serve their student populations, says that for minorities, a year-round school schedule does more than help academically. In an interview with *Education News*, Habash said that schools with high numbers of poor and minority students benefit greatly from year-round schooling because it keeps students on task and leads to more meaningful instruction. When there are not a lot of academically sound options at home, students from disadvantaged backgrounds benefit from the consistency of classroom instruction on a streamlined schedule ("Benefits of Year-Round Schools Touted" n.d.). A recent Congressional Research Service report also found that of year-round school attendees, 75 percent were receiving free or reduced lunches (Mendez 2014).

It is well documented that minorities drop out of high school at rates higher than their white counterparts. The solution to this problem, according to specialists such as Jessica Washington of Politic365, is year-round schooling. She reports that the national dropout rate is 5 percent, while the dropout rate for year-round students is just 2 percent (Washington 2013). These dropout statistics are not broken down by racial or socioeconomic backgrounds, but it stands to reason that if the overall dropout rate is lower for year-round schooling setups, the minority dropout rates in this model are also lower. The reasons dropout rates are lower in year-round setups are easy to deduce: students have less time to adjust to time off from school and, in the case of high schoolers, they do not have the time to take summer jobs.

This inability of teenagers to work and make money in the summer months has actually been cited as a pitfall of year-round schooling. However, I'd argue that the disadvantages of that point are short-lived. High school graduates earn $11,000 more per year than those with a GED or less, and that number rises to $36,000 if they have a bachelor's degree (Breslow 2012). Giving up a few summers of minimum wage work in exchange for the higher lifetime earnings a high school diploma affords is a small price to pay.

It Lessens the Summer Slide

Year-round schooling also means that students do not fall victim to the "summer slide," the well-documented phenomenon in which students can actually unlearn some of the knowledge they worked so hard to attain when too much consecutive time is taken off from school. Research shows that it takes anywhere from eight to thirteen weeks at the beginning of every school year for new teachers to get their students back up to speed and ready to learn the new material (Morin 2016).

The summer fallback disproportionately impacts minority students, students who speak English as a second language, economically disadvantaged students, and students with disabilities. The achievement gap between these academically disadvantaged groups already exists; the summer slide just broadens it. If that wasn't enough to affirm the need for year-round schooling for minorities, researcher Daniel O'Brien concluded that learning proficiency progresses faster for minority students during the school year than for white and economically advantaged students (O'Brien 1999). By implementing year-round schooling, minority and other student groups benefit from the consistent, layered increase of information, without the remedial work cutting into the new school-year schedule.

Closing the achievement gap for minority students is always a central topic of discussion, and it seems to me that we have at least a partial solution right in front of us. Implementing year-round schooling will not only lead to minority students who are more engaged with their academics, but ones who come to rely on the consistency of their educational schedule and are more apt to stick with it.

A survey of school educational decision-makers in 1971 found that 84 percent of respondents felt that year-round schooling would be implemented in all US schools within the next fifteen years (Holzman n.d.). Two districts in San Diego were the first to implement year-round academic calendars, in 1971, and by 1974, thirteen more districts in California followed suit (Von Hipple 2007). Even today, California and its neighbors lead the year-round trend, with four-fifths of all of year-round schedules in the nation in Western states, and over half of them in California. In total, over two million US students attend school on year-round schedules every year, in around three thousand schools in forty-six states (Dessof 2011).

But Won't This Stress Out the Teachers?

There are two common questions related to year-round schooling and teachers. First, does a lack of a season of rejuvenation for educators lead to burnout in the classrooms? Second, how is pay impacted? Let's take a look at these, and other implications, of year-round academic calendars as they relate to teachers.

No Summers Off

Every job comes with its share of headaches and, at one point or another, employees in all industries claim that they are "burned out." Teaching is unique when it comes to burnout, though, because an unmotivated, exhausted teacher has a direct effect on the young people in his or her classroom. Free summers have long been the light at the end of the tunnel for teachers, particularly in urban areas with higher discipline problems and overcrowded classrooms. In a year-round setting, lengthy breaks are gone, replaced with shorter, more frequent ones. Though the loss of those summer months may at first seem like a drawback, many teachers end up liking the greater frequency of time off (Chaika 1999). With shorter, more concentrated spurts of instruction, teachers can exert more energy and face the daily struggles in the knowledge that there will soon be relief. There is still as much time off, but it is more evenly distributed.

More Red Tape

Teachers who work at multi-track year-round schools, or schools that rotate student schedules so time off is staggered and the school is always open, have more work to do. Part of the financial allure of a multi-track schedule is that a school is always at full capacity, which means that teachers share classrooms. "Roving" teachers have to live from carts, or, in some cases, temporary storage, in order to make their classrooms accommodating to other teachers. There are also cases in which a teacher may not get the allotted time off because he or she is changing a grade level or subject and there is no time off between tracks.

Single-track setups have fewer of the issues of multi-track schools, but there are still some conflicts, particularly if the teachers are parents too. If their children go to a traditionally scheduled school, their breaks may not line up and could lead to childcare issues.

The Issue of Pay

In most scenarios, teachers make the same amount of money in their districts whether they work at a year-round or traditional school, though the pay schedules may differ. Teachers who made extra money teaching summer school still have that option in year-round districts that offer remedial courses during break periods. The biggest economic impact for teachers who move to year-round schedules is if they are accustomed to taking on part-time work during the summers. Depending on the type of work, this could mean a loss of several thousand dollars every year. However, for teachers satisfied with holding down just one job and paycheck, a year-round schedule may not have any economic impact on their families at all.

Research has not found any large negative effects on teachers who teach in year-round schedules instead of traditional ones (Chaika 1999). Like any profession, the preferred schedule depends on the individual. For veteran teachers who have been teaching in a traditional setup for years, a switch to year-round schooling may be more jarring than for a newly licensed teacher. Overall, though, the job and time off are comparable—just different.

Can Year-Round Schooling Save the Economy?

Let's now move out and take a look at the overall economic effect of year-round schooling. Does this academic setup help or hurt taxpayers' pockets?

On-Campus Costs and Savings

Year-round school programs are usually based on one of two structures: single-track, which releases all students for breaks throughout the year together, and multi-track, which staggers student breaks and effectively keeps the school building occupied year round. Obviously, on a multi-track schedule, school maintenance costs rise because the building is in full use year round. The cost does not increase by as much as a quarter, though, because most school buildings in a traditional schedule have some employees there in the summer months, and most offer summer school classes for some of that time. Nevertheless, in warm climates, the cost of air conditioning alone can be a deal-breaker when the topic of year-round schooling is broached. There is also the added cost of transportation on more days of school, as well as the salaries of custodial staff and additional administrative staff.

There are some areas where year-round schools can be long-term money-saving options, though. If a particular district has more students than traditional schedules can accommodate, the capital cost of new buildings can be avoided with a multi-track schedule that allows more students to use the same building. Beyond the capital cost of a building, money can be saved because a higher number of students are using the same resources, such as library books or physical-education equipment. Some schools have even listed a decrease in vandalism as a financial plus of year-round occupancy (California Department of Education 2015).

Community Cost and Savings

Each community will feel a different economic impact when it comes to year-round schooling. A tourist community with summer attractions, for example, may feel more of a squeeze if its low-cost employee pool of high school students is suddenly in class instead. The same could be said for ski-resort communities, though those could benefit from multitrack scheduling of high school students during their busiest season. The summer months tend to be when high school students earn the most money, however, because there is a significant period of time with no school responsibilities. Without those months of a steady paycheck, students (and parents) stand to lose potential college money. According to most research, trying to work and maintain a job alongside classes can have a negative impact on grades, and most employers cannot accommodate students who are only available two or three weeks at a time (Lederman 2009).

The potential economic cost of year-round schooling is thus twofold: individual students may suffer financially and local businesses may have to pay more for part-time jobs, which had been ideal for high school students seeking summer employment.

Savings to the community are less tangible, but can be reflected in some research indicating that year-round schooling reduces teen crime, thus saving money for the community (http://www.auburn.edu/~enebasa/html/atrisk_.pp.html). At-risk students tend to perform better in year-round setups, making them more successful in their academic careers, which will lead to a stronger economy down the road if those students avoid dropping out of high school (K12 Academics n.d.). While the savings associated with year-round school schedules may not show up on something as straightforward as a utility bill, they do exist.

Like the impact on students and teachers, the financial ramifications of year-round schooling do not seem to have significant negatives. But for cash-strapped districts, any upfront costs can be a deal-breaker.

Adding More Days to the School Year

In this chapter, I've advocated that K-12 schools shift from the traditional summers-off school calendar to a year-round one. Consistency, less time spent relearning material, and the implications that year-round schooling has for closing the achievement gap are just a few of my reasons for feeling so strongly that this shift take place. There's another piece to this argument, though, and one that deserves a closer look. Along with more evenly splitting up time off, should schools be adding more time to their school days or more total days in the classroom?

A Call for More Time in Classrooms

Our students spend significantly less time in the classroom than students in most other countries. Even President Obama has been vocal about the need for American schools to add more time in the classroom—either through longer school days or by adding more days to the school calendar ("President Obama Wants to Keep Kids in School Longer: Extended Days, Weekend Hours, Shorter Summers" 2009).

Predictably, those comments have received some pushback, both from parents who believe their children are already under too much pressure at school and need every single allotted day off, and from teacher unions that want to know how educators will be properly compensated for the extra time spent in classroom instruction. The idea of adding more time to student school calendars may be unpopular, but that is not reason enough to rule it out.

Is it time to turn the US K-12 school calendar completely on its head by abolishing summers-off schedules and adding time in the classroom? Would such actions make a significant positive impact on student performance, particularly in STEM topics? We'll examine those questions in the coming pages.

But Are All These Days Considered Equal?

Let's look at where American schools rank right now when it comes to days in school versus time off. Thirty states require schools to have a 180-day calendar, two ask for more than 181 school days, and the rest ask for between 171 and 179 days. Minnesota is the only state that has no minimum requirement for number of days students are in the classroom (though the state averages 175 school days). This means that in states with the lowest requirements, students are out of school for more days than they are in it (as many as 194 days per year), a number that contrasts greatly with other developed nations (https://nces.ed.gov/surveys/sass/tables/sass0708_035_s1s.asp.).

Korea has the highest required number of school days, at 225, followed by Japan at 223 and China at 221. Canadian requirements are close to those of the United States, at 188 days, and England is at 190 days. When all developed nations are considered, the international average for days in school is 193—a full two weeks higher than the average for the United States (Fitzgerald 2009).

But are all these days considered equal? How long are the school days in places such as Korea, China, and England? It varies, but it is not uncommon for Korean high school students to spend sixteen hours of each school day in the classrooms. That is more than twice the amount of time that American students spend at school, and is perhaps extreme. Note, though, that Korean students consistently rank at the top of developed nations when it comes to subjects such as math and science, vastly outperforming US students. By contrast, school-aged children in England spend six and a half to seven hours at school—the equivalent of American students (though they spend more days in the classroom) (Burgess 2013).

The Pitfalls of Changing the Status Quo

We have looked at the reasons teachers should get behind the push to support year-round schooling and how more consistent time in the classroom will lead to higher student performance, boosting teacher accountability ratings and accommodating a more streamlined education process. In this section, I want to look at the most common reasons that people are against switching from a summers-off school calendar to a year-round model.

Rising Costs

The summer months are typically the highest for energy consumption. In fact, the average electricity bill for homeowners in the summer months goes up 4 to 8 percent (Rogers 2014). The same would be true for schools. Having empty classrooms in the summer months means less money going to air conditioning and prevents other warm-weather costs from hitting school utility budgets. It may seem like a minor point, but an increase in utility bills for one-quarter of the year could really hurt schools' bottom lines.

Not Enough Downtime

Some childhood-development experts believe that, particularly when it comes to younger students, time off in the summer months is a vital component of healthy development. The argument suggests that kids are not designed to spend so much of their time inside classrooms and that the pleasant summer weather provides a perfect opportunity to get outside and have fun. The problem with this argument, of course, is that most children are not spending their summers frolicking in fields of flowers or running around their neighborhoods, hanging out with other kids.

The days of kids spending their summers outside, communing with nature and getting plenty of exercise are long past. A recent Harvard University study found that school-age children tend to gain weight at a faster pace during the summer months than during the school year, a fact attributed to more time spent in sedentary activities such as watching television or using mobile devices (Adler, Franckle, and Davison 2014). Not only must K-12 students relearn the academic material when they return to the classroom, they must also shift their mentalities from less-active, sedentary ones to sharp, alert learning models—and teachers bear the brunt of this responsibility.

The American Academy of Child and Adolescent Psychiatry reports that by the time children graduate from high school, they will have spent more time watching television than in classrooms ("Watching TV/Screen Time and Children" n.d.). What's more, children who watch an excessive amount of television generally have lower grades in school, read fewer books, and have more health problems. While some children visit summer camps or attend childcare when school is out, others stay at home, inside, with not much else to do than watch TV or play games on electronic devices. This is especially true for kids who are middle-school age or higher and are able to stay home alone when parents work. The "downtime" of the summer months is really just empty time, often void of anything academically or developmentally advantageous.

Scheduling Adjustments

For parents with children of different ages and in different schools, a year-round schedule could present serious scheduling issues. This argument assumes that schools would actually adhere to different time-off schedules—something that seemingly could be adjusted so that all schools within a particular district or geographic area were on the same schedule. It can be difficult for working parents to find babysitters for one or two weeks at a time every few months, as opposed to three months straight in the summer. Again, though, the market tends to adjust to demand. Childcare centers and camps would likely be able to offer programs when students needed them. Just because those programs are not available now does not mean they would not exist if the school schedules shifted.

How to Implement a Year-Round Schooling System in Your School District

In this chapter, we have looked at the pros and cons of year-round schools. Now it is up to you. Do you feel year-round schools would be a good choice for your district? The section that follows offers information on how to transition to a year-round school format, if you choose to go that route.

First, you need to decide what type of year-round school scheduling system you will use. Year-round schools are usually set up as single-track

(ST) with unified attendance or multi-track (MT) with staggered attendance programs. Some schools use a combination of the two. The main difference between the two systems is that single-track allows the entire student and staff population to adhere to the same calendar, and multi-track separates students and teachers and places each in one of several staggered instructional blocks and vacation schedules.

To make this even more complicated, the single-track and multi-track systems can have different variations. In the 60–20 schedule, the school year is separated into three sixty-day sessions with three twenty-day vacations. A variation on this schedule is the 60–15, which provides for an additional three- to four-week collective vacation. This plan can be used with either the single-track or multi-track system. Collectively, these calendars are used by a little more than a third of year-round schools in America.

Lastly, let's talk about two year-round calendars that are used by around 40 percent of year-round schools. In the 45–15 schedule, forty-five days of instruction are followed by fifteen days of vacation time. The related 45–10 schedule provides an additional four-week vacation for staff and students. Again, these plans can be implemented in either a single-track or multi-track systems (Quinlan et al. 1987).

Choosing an Implementation Team

Before attempting to set up a year-round school in your district, it is important to get approval from at least 80 percent of your faculty, staff, and parents. This will require a number of meetings, presentation of literature on the subject, and time for discussion. If you do not get approval, you should strongly reconsider implementing a year-round system in your district. Assuming that you will receive the necessary approval, let's move on to the next steps.

When transitioning to a year-round school setup, you must first assemble the implementation team. Groups no larger than seven usually work best. The team can be made up of a variety of district personnel and staff. Implementation teams normally consist of a school board member, the superintendent and assistant superintendents, principals, teachers, and other pertinent individuals.

Once the team is created, efforts must be made to assess the district's capacity for implementing and sustaining year-round schools. The team must ask itself whether the district has all of the resources needed to implement and sustain a year-round system. In extreme cases, when the district feels it is unable to coordinate its own implementation efforts, the team may want to consider hiring an experienced educational consulting firm to oversee the process. There are many well-qualified firms that will be able to either work in conjunction with an implementation team or oversee the process themselves. Note, however, that this can turn into an enormous job with a significant price tag.

The consulting team or team leader must be committed to developing and implementing innovative strategies that have the potential to effectively produce educational change. Simply assembling a top-notch team is not enough, however. All of the major administrators, including the superintendent and school board, must fully support the decisions of the implementation team.

Remember that parents, community leaders, and policymakers must also be included in the process. Many parents are involved in their students' educational plans and want to be informed of any changes. The implementation team will need to decide if parents and community leaders should be included as formal members of the team, or to simply elicit their advice and expertise as needed. When making decisions concerning which individuals will populate the team, remember to include members who have the expertise to be taken seriously within the district.

Involving parents and community members in the implementation process might provide the restructuring team with a way to engage other members of the community, such as grassroots organizations, local business leaders, and area politicians. Community members can also assist the school in choosing the correct year-round school system and schedule. It is vital for the team to understand the culture of the community, its needs and wants, and the life skills its young people require.

If the school would like to create fundraisers to assist in the efforts to transition to a year-round school system, it is important that the community members understand why the school wants extra money and why they should give the extra money. If the community members disagree with the changes being made, they will be less likely to participate or contribute to the cause.

Having an implementation team is an important component in a successful transition to a year-round school system. The task of choosing the leader and deciding on the roles of the implementation team should not be taken lightly. In many instances, the leader of the implementation team will be the superintendent or someone he or she appoints. Alternatively, the leader and other members of the team can be voted in. The leader must be held accountable for ensuring the success of the entire team as it moves to implement and sustain year-round schooling. The leader's roles might include, but are not restricted to, determining the areas of expertise the team members bring to the table and how he or she can utilize that expertise.

Implementing a Year-Round Schooling System

To ensure the minimum amount of time is spent on implementing the system, the leader will need to establish a standing meeting time and develop an agenda to utilize time to the fullest extent possible. The leader must decide if the team should have mandatory or optional meetings. If the meetings are optional, the leader must decide how information is disseminated to members who do not attend meetings. Prepared agendas are essential for smooth meetings and excellent communication within the team.

Once the year-round system is approved by all team members, the plan will need to be approved by the superintendent before it is presented to the school board. The same rules apply whether implementation is needed by one school or by all the schools in the district.

A concern, alluded to in the comments above, is the need to assess the district's capacity for implementing and sustaining a year-round schooling system. To appropriately assess the abilities of the district or school, the leader will need to complete an inventory of the pros and cons. If the inventory concludes that the district or school does not have the capacity to implement or sustain the plan, it may be wise to suspend the idea until you have the necessary capacity.

Often, volunteer team members do not understand the dedication and length of time it will take to carry out the transition to a year-round schooling schedule. Before the team starts to implement the necessary changes, the leader will need to stress to all team members the enormity of the task, the number of hours the members will need to dedicate to the project, and what is at stake.

Once the team's year-round schooling plan has been approved, it is time to implement the approved plan. First, the implementation team will discuss possible impediments to the approved plan and ensure the team has a contingency plan in place to deal with the issues as they arise. Next, they should implement their target goals and timelines. The leader will need to appoint a member of the implementation team to take on the responsibility of collecting, reporting, and evaluating any data collected. The leader will use the data collected to continuously revise and refine the team's implementation efforts, as well as report their findings to the superintendent and/or the school board.

A useful tool for education specialists considering a move to year-round school years is the "Year-Round Education Program Guide" published by the California Department of Education. The guide takes you through the process of deciding on and implementing a year-round schooling calendar. The steps below are taken from the guide.

Implementation Steps

- Select schools and grade levels.
- Establish a process for resolving issues.
- Select and approve a calendar by working with employee groups.
- Assess the need for facilities modifications, including shade modification and storage areas for off-track teachers.
- Submit budget requests to the district business office.
- Decide if year-round education will be implemented on a voluntary or mandatory basis for students and employees.
- Develop and approve a track preference and assignment policy for students, keeping in mind the need for the same schedules for family members. Balance tracks by ethnicity, academic ability, socioeconomic level, and educational need.
- Develop and approve a track assignment policy for teachers and staff.
- Determine the staff in-service schedule.
- Institute a year-round education informational network for certificated and classified staff members and parents.
- Send choices of tracks to parents by early spring.
- Notify parents as soon as possible of track assignment.

- Develop a policy and system for track-change appeals.
- Develop a system for delivering services during the summer (e.g., classroom supplies and textbooks).
- Modify/expand food services according to need.
- Modify payroll periods.
- Develop a system for plant maintenance and utilization of empty rooms.
- Ensure that air conditioning and insulation are able to provide summer comfort.
- Bargain with all appropriate classified and certificated units.
- Develop a work schedule for office, custodial, and administrative staff members.
- Develop a system to deliver electives and special services, such as special day classes, psychological services, resource specialists, and bilingual education.
- Ensure appropriate cash reserves to meet summer payroll and supply expenses.
- Modify transportation system as required, including routes, number of buses, and service schedules.
- Establish a system for teacher room rotation or roving.
- Develop a community-school communication system for notifying off-track families of important school dates and activities.
- Provide activities for connecting off-track employees and parents.
- Reschedule special events such as holiday programs.
- Design attendance accounting system as required.
- Modify report card schedule.
- Coordinate with community services, such as the recreation department, youth organizations, church groups, and the police department.
- Identify and coordinate with child care providers.
- Identify intersession instructional programs and schedules.
- Modify the student testing program (California Department of Education 2015).

Track Assignment Considerations

General Axioms

Establish the following priorities in deciding who gets first track preference of a track:

- Respect district employees and keep parents on the same track as their children.
- Respect the terms of divorce settlements by respecting parents' visitation schedules.
- Consider unique family circumstances (e.g., predictable annual visits of families located in different parts of the country or the world).
- Acknowledge unique educational opportunities (e.g., a cello prodigy who is offered a summer camp).
- Use a fair, balanced track assignment policy once priorities have been honored. Each track should mirror the ethnic and socioeconomic composition of the entire school population.
- Minimize ability and/or special education need track segregation. If a special population must be put on one track, isolation and segregation can be minimized by partial day integration of self-selection of track.
- Develop an appeals process, including:
  - A site administrator.
  - An appeal committee (made up of an administrator, a teacher, and a board member).

Do not:

- Load tracks by ability level.
- Load tracks by special groups (e.g., band or football).
- Move students from track to track each year (unless requested).
- Wait too long to announce track assignments.

Operational Strategies for Special Services

Special Day Classes

- Typically confined to one track (or two if the population warrants).
- Extended school year days are typically offered during intersessions (California Department of Education 2015).

Evaluation of a Year-Round Schooling System

In order to validate their efforts, the implementation team will need to evaluate the effectiveness of its year-round schooling system. The process of evaluation can be completed in-house, or the district can hire outside consultants to perform the task. Hiring outside consultants is preferable, as it provides an impartial evaluation of the year-round schools. However, this can be costly, so many school districts may have no choice but to do it themselves. If the implementation team is willing to evaluate the success of the year-round school system, they must first develop a plan for evaluation.

The team's evaluation plan should have been developed before the year-round schooling system was implemented. Performance goals that were created at the beginning of the implementation process should be used to guide the evaluation process. The team will need to decide who will collect, analyze, and interpret the data. In order to avoid biased results, it may be in the best interests of the school to hire an outside consultant who may provide a more objective assessment. The team will also use the results to determine whether the year-round schooling system was effective. The results may indicate that the plan was not a success. In this case, the best solution is to build upon the small successes and learn from the mistakes.

Implementation of a year-round school system is a long-term process. Reform occurs on a continuous cycle that must be sustained in order for improvements to be maintained and furthered. Keep in mind that not every reform effort bears fruit. Even the best schools have to continue to work in order to perfect their year-round schooling system.

Concluding Thoughts

In this chapter, we explored how students' experiences can be enhanced by implementing a year-round schooling system. Year-round schools can offer students more engagement, more learning time, and shorter downtime during which learning may be lost. Year-round programs can be especially beneficial for low-income and minority children, who have been statistically shown to suffer most from long school breaks. Students who need more time to learn may benefit from extra help teachers are able to provide when increased school time allows them to do so. Increasing the time spent in school would bring the US education system more in line with other developed countries, helping our children to be better prepared to compete in a global community.

While a major advantage of year-round schools is more quality instruction time, the administration of year-round schools requires extra effort when it comes to managing students, teachers, and the structural requirements of the school. Schools may find it expensive and challenging to manage the cost of extended day education. Clearly, year-round schools have some disadvantages; however, research shows that as parents, students, and teachers grow accustomed to year-round schooling systems, they inevitably find it more satisfactory when compared to schools operating under traditional school calendars.

To enable our children to be truly competitive in the global marketplace, and to give them the opportunities that they need to succeed, our educational system needs to grow and change. Year-round schooling should be strongly considered as one part of the answer to better educating America's youth.

References

Adler, Rachel, Rebecca Franckle, and Kirsten Davison. 2014. "Accelerated Weight Gain among Children during Summer versus School Year and Related Racial/Ethnic Disparities: A Systematic Review." *Preventing Chronic Disease*, 11, 130355. Accessed September 9, 2016. http://dx.doi.org/10.5888/pcd11.130355.

American Academy of Child and Adolescent Psychiatry. n.d. "WatchingTV/Screen Time and Children." Accessed September 9, 2016. http://www.

aacap.org/AACAP/Families_and_Youth/Facts_for_Families/FFF-Guide/Children-And-Watching-TV-054.aspx.

"Benefits of Year-Round Schools Touted." n.d. *Education News*. Accessed September 9, 2016. http://www.educationnews.org/articles/benefits-of-year-round-schools-touted.html.

Breslow, Jason. 2012. "By the Numbers: Dropping Out of High School." *PBS Frontline*. Accessed September 9, 2016. http://www.pbs.org/wgbh/frontline/article/by-the-numbers-dropping-out-of-high-school/.

Burgess, Matt. 2013. "Mapped: How Many Hours Do Children Spend at School around the World?" Help Me Investigate. Accessed September 9, 2016. http://helpmeinvestigate.com/education/2013/04/mapped-how-many-hours-do-children-spend-at-school-around-the-world/.

California Department of Education. 2015. "Year-Round Education Program Guide." Accessed September 9, 2016. http://www.cde.ca.gov/ls/fa/yr/guide.asp.

Chaika, Gloria. 1999. "Is Year-Round Schooling the Answer?" *Education World*. Accessed September 9, 2016. http://www.educationworld.com/a_admin/admin/admin137.shtml.

Dessoff, Alan. 2011. "Is Year-Round Schooling on Track? Summer Learning Loss and Overcrowding Drive Alternative Schedules." *District Administration*. Accessed September 9, 2016. https://www.districtadministration.com/article/year-round-schooling-track.

Fitzgerald, John. 2009. "Minnesota School Year Requirements Too Casual." *Minnesota 2020*. Accessed September 9, 2016. http://www.mn2020.org/issues-that-matter/education/minnesota-school-year-requirements-too-casual.

Holzman, Seymour. n.d. "Year-Round School: Districts Develop Successful Programs." Education USA. Accessed September 9, 2016. http://eric.ed.gov/?id=ED062682.

K12 Academics. n.d. "Education Policy: Advantages." Accessed September 9, 2016. http://www.k12academics.com/education-policy/year-round-school/advantages#.V9VFZ_krLDd.

Lederman, Doug. 2009. "The Impact of Student Employment." *Inside Higher Ed*. Accessed September 9, 2016. https://www.insidehighered.com/news/2009/06/08/work.

Mendez, Edgar. 2014. "Congressional Report Highlights Year-Round Schools." *Milwaukee Journal-Sentinel*, July 8. Accessed September 9, 2016. http://archive.jsonline.com/blogs/news/266264841.html.

Morin, Amanda. 2016. "The Pros and Cons of Year-Round Schooling." *Child Parenting*. Accessed September 9, 2016. http://childparenting.about.com/od/schoollearning/a/year-round-school-pros-cons.htm.

O'Brien, Daniel M. 1999. "Family and School Effects on the Cognitive Growth of Minority and Disadvantaged Elementary Students." University of Texas at Dallas. Accessed September 9, 2016. http://www.utdallas.edu/research/tsp-erc/pdf/wp_obrien_1999_family_school_affects.pdf.

"President Obama Wants to Keep Kids in School Longer: Extended Days, Weekend Hours, Shorter Summers." 2009. *NY Daily News*, September 28. Accessed September 9, 2016. http://www.nydailynews.com/news/national/president-obama-kids-school-longer-extended-days-weekend-hours-shorter-summers-article-1.407418.

Quinlan, Claire, George, Cathy and Emmett, Terry. 1987. *Year-Round Education: Year-Round Opportunities: A Study of Year-Round Education in California*. Los Angeles, CA: California State Department of Education.

Rogers, Kate. 2014. "How to Keep Your Electricity Bills Cool This Summer." *Fox Business*. Accessed September 9, 2016. http://www.foxbusiness.com/features/2014/05/27/how-to-keep-your-electricity-bills-cool-this-summer.html.

Von Hipple, Paul. 2007. "Save Iowa Summers." Accessed September 9, 2016. http://www.saveiowasummers.com/wp-content/uploads/2010/07/Paul-von-Hipple-Research1.pdf.

Washington, Jessica. 2013. "Year-Round School Could Be the Answer to the Minority Drop-Out Problem." *Politic365*. Accessed September 9, 2016. http://politic365.com/2013/05/20/year-round-school-could-be-the-answer-to-the-minority-drop-out-problem/.

Examining the Present and Future of K-12 Assessments

- Accountability in public education: The necessities and pitfalls of assessments.
- Where assessments stand today: A look at the current situation in our public schools.
- Problems with Common Core: Is Common Core the panacea we were promised? What went wrong?
- Greater focus on how to obtain knowledge: Moving on from memorizing facts and into correct research methods.
- More critical-thinking options: Improvements in critical thinking will boost writing and math skills.
- Higher levels of digital access: We live in a digital world. Students need to have access to and learn how to use computers and online resources.
- Better assessments based on cultural and learning differences: Tailoring assessments so all students have equal access.

Ankur Singh, a student at the University of Missouri—Columbia, took an English class in his junior year of high school that influenced him profoundly. "It was the only class I've ever taken where the lessons I learned will carry with me for the rest of my life, and after completion I felt ten times smarter," he says. The teacher focused on the development of the students' critical-thinking skills and ensured that they were able to analyze poems and essays. He was keen to allow each student to form his or her own opinions.

    Because Singh loved the junior-year English class so much, he expected the college-prep AP English course he enrolled in during his senior year would be equally enjoyable. However, it turned out to be an awful experience. The critical-thinking skills he had honed the previous year were of no use in the new class; instead, the class focused solely on preparing them for the inevitable exam. "It frustrated me to no avail and I ended up doing very poor in AP English," Singh says. "And I found the exact same thing in all of my other AP classes, which seemed more focused on college preparation and standardized tests rather than genuine learning."

Singh began to wonder what the real purpose of education was. "All around me were students studying diligently, stressing out about their grades, homework, the ACT, college essays, AP tests. And here I was not really caring about any of those things. Were there really no students in this school who wanted anything more than just a college degree and a job?" He began to feel lonely, and then angry. Finally, during an AP French exam, he used the time to write a furious letter to the College Board, expressing his misgivings. Though he expected to be reprimanded by his French teacher for writing a letter rather than taking the exam, she listened sympathetically and told him that she felt the same frustrations with the system. Though she had wanted to take the French students on field trips to a French bakery or watch a French film, she was forced to teach to the test. "Maybe if the students themselves spoke out against it," she said, "it could all change" (Strauss 2012).

As Ankur Singh's story demonstrates, the current model of assessments can lead to frustration in students and teachers alike. In this chapter we will look at the use of effective assessment measures in determining a student's abilities and academic potential.

Accountability in Public Education

In the US public-school system, there is a lot of talk of "accountability." Teachers are held accountable for what their students do or do not know. Administrators are taken to task if standardized test scores are too low, or drop from one year to the next. State lawmakers are asked to correct any "crisis" of underperforming students through legislation. When it comes to the progress and success of our K-12 students, the ball is constantly being passed, until some course of action is put in place that will presumably fix whatever academic woe is perceived in a particular school, district, or state.

One major way that this accountability is enforced is through standardized testing. By applying the same requirements to each teacher and student within a state, the general theory is that accountability for student success will be upheld. Truly understanding what our students are learning is more complicated than that, though. The dismal state of today's K-12 assessments is one of the biggest reasons our public schools are failing their students.

We also measure the success of K-12 systems in the United States through graduation rates and through college acceptance and graduation numbers. These only tell part of the story, however. Presumably, handing someone a diploma means that person has mastered the required material and "knows" what is needed to earn the graduation distinction.

We know that American students lag behind other developed countries when it comes to math and science achievement. Students in countries such as South Korea and Singapore consistently outrank US students when it comes to basic and advanced math and science achievements (Rich 2012). Survey after survey of business leaders bemoan the lack of basic writing and communication skills their employees possess (Nolop 2013), and on the 2011 National Assessment of Educational Progress, only 27 percent of twelfth graders were proficient in writing (Leal 2012).

If we wait until students are done with K-12 learning to figure out if they are learning what they need to know, we will be too late. Assessments throughout the K-12 journey are necessary, but how those assessments are administered is one of the most hotly contested issues surrounding the K-12 system today.

The "teach to the test" mentality has become the bane of every K-12 educator's existence. Even teachers who are strongly opposed to such a narrow way of educating students find that staying within a narrow realm of material becomes a necessity in the contemporary classroom. Increasingly, the worth of teachers is being derived from student performance results, and specifically standardized testing. The entire value of what a teacher does in a classroom during a given year, and how the teachers performed in prior years, often boils down to what a statewide blanket test spits out in the way of student results. While benchmarks for grade levels have merit, the way that assessments are administered and weighted in today's K-12 public schools are ineffective and unfair to the teachers who must adhere to them.

Frances Banales, president of the Tucson Education Association, highlights the stresses involved in teaching to the test. The stress, she says, emerges from "the idea that we are not doing what's best for kids." She adds: "The anxiety can lead you to question the profession you are dedicated to. . . . You're testing, not instructing. You have to draw on all your strength. There's a lot of preparation a teacher has to do to administer the test. You have to present a calm supportive atmosphere" (Overman n.d.).

According to Banales, the stresses surface in various ways. Some teachers shut down, becoming more robotic in their teaching. Some talk more, while others show their stress by becoming quieter. She notes that some teachers don't eat enough during the weeks of testing, and the stresses inevitably affect the teachers' home lives: "You have to do so much that you end up not having time for your personal family life. You have to get everything in; you're trying to really prioritize" (Overman n.d.).

And, of course, it is not only the teachers who are stressed. Students as well are under tremendous pressure to succeed. As Banales notes: "They give up. They may literally not read through the [test] questions. They get angry or sick. They act out" (Overman n.d.).

Despite having qualms over the basics of standardized testing, many educators view it as a necessary evil of the improvement process. More cynical educators view it as a completely useless process that is never a true indicator of what students actually know. Proponents of K-12 assessments say that without them, there is no adequate way to enforce educator accountability and to truly ascertain if students are learning what they should know at each level. Critics say that assessments put too much focus on a narrow span of information and force teachers to teach to the test, thus leading to rampant anti-intellectualism. Is rote memorization a true test of the knowledge of students? If teachers are given too much freedom, will students acquire the basic knowledge? These and other questions need to be addressed in order to build a stronger educational system in the United States.

Where Assessments Stand Today

Assessments of K-12 students are state developed and mandated at this point, but there is still plenty of federal oversight. While the federal government cannot tell a state what exactly to cover in an assessment, it can make certain subjects and benchmarks more attractive. Federal funding through programs such as the Obama administration's Race to the Top are tied to assessment scores in specific areas, such as math or science learning. Thus, the states that choose to include these federally friendly standards do so, at least partially, with financial incentives in mind. States are rewarded based on the students who achieve standards in areas that the federal government sees as priorities (White House n.d.).

Having national standards is not the problem; incentivizing those standards is. We all learn from a young age that every person is unique and that no two people are alike. Educators learn that students have different learning styles and different strengths when it comes to those learning styles. A country such as the United States, established on the principles of individual liberties and life goals, should be especially open-minded when it comes to nuances between the students in its public schools.

Yet assessments seem to take these basic ideals and throw them out the window, blanketing all students with a set of standards to which they must adhere. Not only must students all be on the same page when it comes to this learning; their teachers must treat them as identical when it comes to the education process. Based on the ideology alone, standardized assessments are flawed. When they are then put into practice, their weaknesses are revealed. How can all students be measured with the same yardstick, and how can punishments and rewards be handed out using such a scale?

Enter Common Core Standards. No education policy and reform on a national scale has received more attention and vitriol than the Common Core Standards, which have been implemented in over forty states. Though Common Core benchmarks were developed through a consortium of states, their perceived association with national politics is heightened.

The basics of Common Core standards are more critical-thinking requirements, a higher emphasis on math and science proficiency, and better career-readiness initiatives in all pursuits (Common Core State Standards Initiative 2013).

These standards are, naturally, assessed through standardized testing. In the case of Common Core, it is through the Partnership for Assessment of Readiness for College and Careers (PARCC) testing. These results are used to determine progress and outline areas for improvement in K-12 schools. Basically, every educational initiative should be examined and weighed based on its contribution to the future college and career goals of the student at hand. The lingering question then becomes: are learning experiences irrelevant if they are not directly related to college placement and career advancement? (Core Standards 2013)

The standards-based Common Core approach to education reform has already been attacked for its disconnection to what kids should really know and what they are simply required to regurgitate for the sake of a test—déjà vu from the early days of NCLB. Parents who see their children struggling with the heightened intensity of the standards have taken to social media and blogs to complain, and conservative groups that believe states are overstepping their educational power have petitioned their governors to withdraw their states from the standards.

There is plenty of misinformation floating around about Common Core Standards, their origination, and states' roles in administering them. To understand what these standards and any future standards with a national push mean, we first have to know exactly what they are.

Contrary to what many may think, Common Core standards were not developed by the federal government, or any particular presidential administration. Common Core standards are the creation of the Governors' Association and were developed with input from many states before they were finalized. From there, states could decide whether to implement the standards or not—there was never a mandate to accept them.

Nearly every state was on board to implement Common Core standards when they were first released. However, some states have since lost that fervor, with Indiana being the first one to renege on its original decision and opt out of Common Core after just one year of implementation. South Carolina and Oklahoma quickly followed suit. The reasons behind these flip-flops were obscure. Officially, the governors of these states said they decided to go with standards that better addressed the needs of their specific student bodies. Unofficially, critics of the governors' moves said they were simply political actions intended to gain favor with constituents who were anti-Common Core, and particularly those who felt that the standards were associated with President Obama (which they never were) (Core Standards 2013).

Regardless of why states decided against Common Core, either at the outset or after implementation, they remain in the majority of classrooms across the country. So what exactly *are* the Common Core benchmarks, and why are they viewed as being so groundbreaking and controversial?

In a nutshell, the Common Core Standards put a stronger focus on areas where American students typically fall behind: math, science, and engineering. They set a higher bar for learning in these areas, along with language arts and critical thinking. And while the federal government played no implementation role, it did back the standards to the point of offering financial incentives for states that adopted them (Race to the Top is an example of this). By agreeing to the standards set forth by Common Core, states were in essence agreeing to the nationalization of learning benchmarks for the betterment of the K-12 student population as a whole.

Problems with Common Core

Setting uniform standards for students from South Dakota to New York City sounds like a smart plan in theory. In order to compete in the future world economy, American students need to master certain subject areas and be on the same page with them. The standardization of learning also helps feed the college system more readily, ensuring that students are learning at a heightened level and not being taught remedial skills that should have been mastered before high school graduation. However, as noted earlier, the way these blanket standards are measured for effectiveness is through assessments. Once again, each state has its own brand of assessments, but those that have adopted Common Core standards must adhere to a heightened level of questioning.

The problems with Common Core standards and their accompanying assessments lie below the surface, and reflect the larger problems with K-12 testing in America. No two students are the same. When you factor in things such as environmental and socioeconomic differences, as well as regional environments, there really is no way that any one curriculum standard or set of tests can cover an entire nation of K-12 learners (or even a majority of them, based on the states that have adopted the standards). Assessments turn living, breathing students into machines, who must be programmed to spit out the right answers at the right time.

Common Core standards thrust the issue of what should be learned, and how that material should be tested, into the national spotlight again. While educators had never abandoned this discussion, and likely never will, the general public seemed to awaken abruptly and passionately when confronted with the topic of what K-12 students should be learning. This has set the stage for a thorough reimagining of assessments in US classrooms and has presented an opportunity for public support of change. So where do we start? In the sections that follow, we will discuss strategies that can be used by education professionals to develop assessments of the future and focus these assessment on what matters most—student learning.

Greater Focus on *How* to Obtain Knowledge

In this digital age, there is more information available than can ever be processed, and it is crucial that students learn how to vet this data. While the internet has opened up the world in amazing and beautiful ways, it has also skewed the way information is obtained. Instant knowledge, or perceived knowledge, is available as soon as kids are old enough to type in a password or swipe a screen. The internet has eliminated the information exploration process in many ways, with search engine providers racing to spoon feed people the precise answers they need.

For those who grew up in the pre-internet days, the idea of simply Googling the answer for our homework is mind-boggling. However, a baby girl born today will likely be the star of an entire Facebook photo album before she is even one day old. Her milestone moments of early childhood will be plastered on the Facebook, Twitter, and Instagram feeds of her doting parents, and by the time she is a toddler, there will be at least a few smartphone or tablet apps that belong to her on her parents' devices. Her life will be an open book in many respects, chronicled for her own parents' posterity but also shared with a world of close friends and not-so-close acquaintances. By the time she starts kindergarten, she will have spent thousands of hours staring at screens. Technology will be a part of life.

There is no way to take away the technology experiences that kids have before they even enter our public K-12 classrooms, and we shouldn't seek to do that. However, it does change the way this generation of K-12 students will approach the pursuit of knowledge and it is vastly different from previous ones. Perhaps just as important as the actual facts our students learn is making sure they are correctly obtaining that knowledge. Assessments are one way to check up on this goal.

Assessments of the future will need to ask more questions about the *how* of knowledge and not just focus on the *what*. There is no longer one set of books that answers a particular set of questions, and even materials as traditional as US history books are coming under scrutiny for being too one dimensional.

These issues have come to the fore in Texas, where a battle rages regarding the inclusion of alternative versions of American history textbooks in high schools. More than fifty organizations and a coalition of

Hispanic-American educators in the state petitioned the Texas State Board of Education to allow alternative history as an elective for high school students. The petitioners were not asking to change the traditional textbooks; they merely wanted to add more perspectives to the learning process for those who wished to do so. The petition was denied, ostensibly because of cost concerns, but certain board members admitted that they feared leftist ideals entering history textbooks (Wang 2016).

Politics aside, the debate in Texas brings up some other interesting points about how exactly this generation of K-12 students obtains knowledge. Disallowing the alternative histories in classrooms does not cut off student access; it simply directs them to unauthorized versions that can be created, and posted online, by anyone. This is true for any topic. Students have all of the information they will ever need at the tips of their fingers, and they will grow up never knowing what life was like pre-internet. They don't need to go to the library or to check a few sources before determining the true answer—they just need a smartphone. This presents a slippery slope for educators, who have been told to embrace the very technology that often misinforms their students. Not all free information, particularly online, is created equal. More than ever, educators need to show students how to find the answers on their own. This process of finding information should vary from school to school in order to adjust to the populations using it, but should contain these features:

An Online Vetting Process

How can students know if what they are reading is reliable? They should be taught to consider the source. Government publications, large trusted nonprofit names, and some newspapers should make the list of acceptable websites (though even these should be carefully considered). Students should be encouraged to compare various online sources (such as Wikipedia, the *New York Times*, and Fox News) on a particular topic, and evaluate the factual information. Since some editorial content is now going the way of paid content, otherwise known as native advertising, sites with an interest in making money (including some "news" publications) should be examined with a skeptical eye. As advertising online continues to evolve, so too should the way we examine the content we consume—and students should be a part of that process. Students should know how to spot unbiased, reliable information and separate that from misleading content. That skill starts with vetting the source, and looking for clues in the content that point to reliability, instead of simply taking what is presented at face value.

Instruction in the Basics

Though actual books on shelves are rapidly disappearing, the information housed in our school, university, and public libraries is still an important cornerstone of learning, particularly when students are searching for information. Our students should know the difference between a Wikipedia page and a peer-reviewed article on the same topic. They should understand reference books and where to find the information contained within them—whether that is a physical library shelf or a specific website.

Investigating Multiple Sources

The instant gratification of the internet has provided a shortcut for today's students when it comes to research and obtaining knowledge. Answers are quite literally at the tips of their fingers and easy to insert in any assignment. Students should question what they read, however, even if the sources seem reliable. A benefit of the internet is that there is more than one side to every story, which means that today's students should be handing in well-rounded work that contains more than one piece of information. Even the "facts" surrounding our Founding Fathers and other pieces of American history are being scrutinized more closely than before, in part because of the vast reach of the internet. Students should be encouraged to seek out more than one avenue when it comes to the learning process and should use that information to formulate a well-rounded response to any assignment.

An Understanding of Internet-Related Ethics

Today's students do not need to write answers on the insides of their hands or pay another student to write their research papers in order to cheat academically. In many cases all they need is a cell phone, a search engine, and sometimes a credit card. With so much information available at the touch of a button, student understanding of what is cheating when it comes to finding answers can be murky.

Recently, one of the most lauded public schools in New York, Stuyvesant High, was caught in a massive cheating scandal. The cheating was discovered when school authorities confiscated the cell phone of a sixteen-year-old during an exam. Scouring the phone, officials realized they'd stumbled on a huge cheating network. The students had been passing photographs of the text pages to each other. Sixty-nine students were nabbed in the subsequent investigation; all would have to retake the exams.

The Stuyvesant High scandal caught the attention of the nation because of its stature; however, it was by no means an outlier. Similar activity in a Houston school during an English exam let to disciplinary action for sixty students. And cheating on an SAT test at a Long Island school led to national changes in the how authorities administered the test.

A recent graduate of Stuyvesant, Madeline S. Rivera, felt that social networking had created an upsurge in cheating, and said: "I can assure you it is pretty much the same at every other high school" (Baker 2012). A Common Sense Media survey discovered that at least 35 percent of students had cheated on assignments via cell phone (Common Sense Media 2009)—though many of those respondents were unaware that what they had done was ethically questionable. Some ways that students cheat to find their answers include texting answers to other students, storing notes on their cell phones, rewriting information found online, using virtual assistant programs to find answers, and flat-out paying online companies to write papers or complete assignments for them. In many cases, it does not even occur to the students that they are doing anything unethical. To them, they are just finding the answers to the questions presented in the most efficient way. This reliance on the quickest, most accessible information is dangerous to the academic futures of K-12 students, and educators should fight against it through policy and discussion. Students may have to unlearn the information-gathering tactics that have been built in from birth.

How do we assess this information-gathering process? It is one thing for teachers to align their lesson plans with these methods; it is another to be able to tell which students have mastered them. We require a separate assessment that focuses solely on the process of information seeking—whether it is in included in assessments that are already written, or given as a test at certain benchmarks in the K-12 career. The optimal time would be midway through the elementary career (third grade) and then again in sixth grade, ninth grade, and twelfth grade. These tests should be graded individually by each teacher.

In lieu of an actual "test," these skills might be assessed in the way of a class project. Research papers and other long-term projects are certainly not new to a teacher's agenda, but the "assessment" side of this information gathering would have specific requirements for the intended outcomes, listed above. Guiding the way our students obtain knowledge will impact every other fact or piece of knowledge and needs to be a required piece of K-12 learning—and then tested.

More Critical-Thinking Options

Applied knowledge is crucial to the learning process, and our standardized tests need to do a better job of measuring it. Every child needs to be able to articulate what he or she knows, not just repeat it. While it may not be as efficient to grade answers that go beyond filling in a bubble, these are the questions students need to answer in order to apply their knowledge in real-world applications. Instead of simply finding the answer, students need to explain their thought process.

What exactly is critical thinking and how does it play into our K-12 classrooms? Do educators really understand the concept? According to Richard Paul (2004), most educators do not actually understand what critical thinking entails and are therefore unable to teach it to their students.

Paul speaks specifically to the lack of critical thinking in college classrooms and how faculty there are often unable to teach it adequately. However, as we all know, the students who show up in college classrooms are products of our K-12 environments. Young adulthood is too late to teach the basic tenets of critical thinking. For one thing, students have by then already figured out all of their academic shortcuts. Many have learned how to rig the academic system in their favor. By college age, students have mastered the K-12 structure that earned them a high school diploma and are eager to apply those habits in higher education. However, critical-thinking skills need to be taught and properly assessed long before that first college course and well before college graduates are in the workforce (Elder and Paul 2012).

Critical thinking improves writing and communication skills. By ensuring that more critical thinking and explanation standards are written into assessments, teachers are guaranteeing that students can explain what they know both in the classroom and in real life.

One of the most difficult tasks toward really changing our K-12 classrooms into critical-thinking hubs is the traditional teacher-student model. Historically, classroom learning has been a one-way conversation in which students were talked "at" and not "with." Students were expected to sit politely, behave, and do the work asked of them. A student who questioned the presented material might be viewed as disruptive or even mean-spirited. While there are certainly students who act out in class simply to get attention or avoid their schoolwork, this traditional setup has caused students to be less-active participants in their educations. It has taken learning empowerment away from students who are conditioned to simply believe what they are told, complete the work, and keep their heads down.

Classrooms today are much more interactive than they were even a decade ago (LaBree 2016). Nevertheless, the "teacher knows best" mentality lingers and gets in the way of students taking an active role in what they are learning and how they are learning it. When you factor in high-stakes testing and its implications for the careers of teachers, funneling vast amounts of information in that one-way conversation style often seems like the only viable approach for teachers. For many teachers, there is a lacuna between the way they want to teach and the way they are forced to teach. This is primarily due to unreasonable accountability standards that include student performance on standardized tests.

We should strive to reach a point where teachers are no longer afraid to stop and take questions on a certain topic, or to entertain a counter view on a topic from a student for the sake of classroom discussion because they are worried about losing time on test-related material. Students who not only master the material, but can evaluate it for themselves and come to their own conclusions on how it will impact their lives, should be able to pass any assessment with flying colors. We just need to decide as an educational community that critical-thinking components are vital to the learning process, and that taking the time to include them in our testing process does more good to our students than simply filling in a multiple-choice bubble. Teaching our students that it is okay to question and doubt and take the time to agree with the answers will go a long way toward creating future generations of critical thinkers.

Given the above, what should critical-thinking options look like in assessments? The Common Core Standards already emphasize more of a hands-on approach to classroom learning, and those values are reflected in the accompanying tests (Core Standards 2013). A good example of a critical-thinking exercise for a third grader would be to not just simply rehash the plot of a story but to draft an email that one character would likely write to another. In this example, the student is taking the knowledge presented and extending it to include his or her own thoughts on the story. In the reading portion of assessments, activities such as this should be asked of the test takers. Comprehension is still important, of course, but alongside the basics of what is read should be proof that the student truly understood the material and can not only regurgitate it, but can interpret it beyond what is on the page.

In areas such as math, critical thinking is also important. Numbers on a page tend to feel somewhat removed from the human experience. Critical-thinking exercises should breathe new life into those numbers and allow students to find a way to incorporate the information in daily life. A student should be able not just to show his or her work but explain why a certain solution was reached and what math concept it demonstrates. There also needs to be more cohesion between different areas of math to show that it is not as cut and dry as it seems and that all of the concepts are interrelated. Our math assessments need to reflect more of the process of reaching math goals, and place less emphasis on the final answer.

The critical-thinking element should be incorporated in the teaching of all subjects, not just language arts and math. Traditionally, the assessment process has been heavy on answers and light on the processes to get there. That is starting to change. More teachers and administrators are recognizing that a fuller grasp of critical-thinking processes is necessary to the improve K-12 classrooms and the next generation of adults.

Higher Levels of Digital Access

All facets of education are being impacted by the rapid evolution of technology, and assessments are not immune. Not only should educators be able to tap into digital resources for assessment preparation, but students should be able to take assessments using the technology that makes them most comfortable. In other words, we need to ditch the Scantron forms and No. 2 pencils and give our kids access to the right technology to make them comfortable with the tests they are taking, and to streamline the process for scorers. There is value in the handwritten word, but this generation of K-12 students will not be handing in business reports or notes scribbled in pencil on college-ruled paper. Our kids should learn to type early on, and should use the wide array of technology at their fingertips for the learning process. Assessments should reflect that shift.

To those outside the educational community, the idea that students should be able to take tests through computers is a no-brainer. Yet within the educational community there is always some fretting when it comes to anything related to technology. For decades, classroom assessments have been done in quiet classrooms with individual test packets and students filling in bubbles on scan sheets with sharpened pencils. In recent years, there have been added sections for free thought that exists outside of multiple-choice responses, but the tests are virtually the same as they were when many of us took our own standardized tests as K-12 students. Changing the format of how these tests are delivered is a scary proposition for many lawmakers and administrators, and comes with a hefty price tag. When you add in the voices of educators who are leery of technology takeovers in classrooms, it isn't difficult to see why there is so much handwringing when it comes to updating the way that assessments are delivered. Nevertheless, it is important to find a financial way to make the technology of assessments possible.

There are several schools of thought when it comes to what kids should be learning in our K-12 schools. Some believe all activities should be focused on getting students ready for the real world and should point to career-readiness programs. Why waste time in the classroom on lofty ideas or benchmarks that have no adaptation to real life? Others believe that there should be at least some inclusion of intellectual pursuits for their own sake. Not everything learned in a K-12 classroom needs a direct relationship with something in the real world that will benefit our students monetarily down the road. Some learning is simply important to developing better humans who pass along that cultural knowledge to the next generations.

It is our job to ensure students have adequate access to and mastery of the technology that will be part of their everyday lives as adults. Wherever possible, technology should be incorporated into our lesson plans and used in our classrooms because it will make a difference in how well versed this generation of students will be across subject dividing lines.

Integrating higher levels of technology in assessments, whether the state-mandated versions or even just in-classroom ones, will have two positive results. The first is that they will reinforce students' use of technology by asking them to implement it to take the actual tests. The second is that assessments will make more sense in the grand scheme of classroom learning, which is already much more interactive than the traditional test-taking process that is still used in standardized assessments. Students who take tests on computers or tablets will be more comfortable with the material at hand and it will feel like they are participating in more of an integrated process. Rather than protesting against the technologizing of education, educators need to insist that technology be part of not only the teaching process, but also of assessment policy.

Better Assessments Based on Cultural and Learning Differences

Not all students are natural test takers. Any educator who has spent even a small amount of time in classrooms knows this—just as students have different learning styles, they have varying test-taking abilities. Most teachers are able to deal effectively with these discrepancies. Even if the teachers do not adjust the tests or assignments from one year to the next, their general demographic remains the same based on location. Inner-city math teachers, for example, might include word problems that relate to the students entering their classrooms and stay away from obscure references. A science teacher in an elite prep school could do the same, using references that strike a chord with the students.

Statewide assessments don't have that level of customization. They are created for one set of students and are then applied to the rest. A student who feels isolated from the material will not be as successful in answering the questions. Those who speak English as a second language, for example, may not perform as well on assessment tests as their peers. Standardized assessments make many assumptions about those who are taking them, and often cater to a particular socioeconomic group of students. For assessments to really be effective, the background of the student answering the questions should always be considered.

What sorts of cultural differences should be considered when assessments are created?

Socioeconomic Status

Students from homes where one or both parents have a college education tend to have more advanced linguistic capabilities. Accomplishing school tasks comes more easily to them than to students from economically disadvantaged homes. This is not to say that test questions should be easier or in any way "dumbed down" based on the income of a family in question, but assessments should be carefully written with these factors in mind. If all students had the chance to take tests that played to their socioeconomic strengths, and avoided pitfalls that made that student feel isolated from the material, we would see a drastic change in test scores. Considering the socioeconomic status of students is an important part of the assessment process that needs to be addressed in order for all students to succeed.

Language

The language spoken at home should be a factor in the type of assessment students receive. Students who speak English as a second language, even fluently, should have the option to take their assessments in whatever language makes them the most comfortable. There should never be a debate about whether a student knows "enough" of the English language to perform well on an assessment. If there is even a question, the student should be given the test in his or her native language, or at least asked for the preference. If we are truly trying to gauge what these students know, we should not force them to battle the language barrier to present that knowledge. Students should be allowed to request tests in whatever language makes them the most comfortable—no questions asked, and no hoops to jump through.

Learning Style

This one is a little more complicated to implement and possibly a pipe dream at this point in the assessment reform process. A *perfect* assessment system would allow students to answer questions in a way that complemented their personalities and learning styles. Teachers could help determine this through their own observations of the students. The trick would be to ensure that all the material was equally difficult and that the students were placed with the right test based on their learning style. A student who did well in traditional test taking, for example, may actually perform worse in a testing environment that was tailored to visual or hands-on learners. This type of assessing would need some trial and error to get right, but could end up yielding big results in student test success. It's something that would need a lot more research and testing before implementation but I believe it would be worth the effort to reach a point of truly fair and accurate assessments.

One of the strongest arguments against standardized assessments is that they are just that—standardized. To really give a full picture of what students are learning, assessments need to be customized to fit students' life circumstances and personalities. It is contradictory to say that American public schools embrace students from all backgrounds, at all learning levels, and with every personality type, but then to test one model student who is not an accurate representation of any of them. This doesn't further our educational pursuits, and it certainly does not further the academic success of the students who take the tests. Blanket assessments are not an accurate representation of a teacher's strengths. By trying to accommodate the masses, assessments have left the individuals behind and the result is a system of testing that does nothing to help anyone in the process and contributes little to what we know about actual student progress.

As they exist today, standardized assessments are ineffective and misleading. By adjusting tests to meet the individual needs of the students taking them, the assessments would at least stand a chance of affecting the lives of the students who take them. It may be impossible to tailor each test to the needs of the student who will take it, but as technology improves, the tools will exist to make this at least partially a reality. Consider a future in which teachers are able to type in information about a student and then receive a customized test based on that information. We have the technology through our smartphones that tells us right down to the grocery store aisle what is for sale—surely there is a developer out there who can create the same type of targeting for test making. We should be able to create tests that will most benefit our students and give educators the most accurate picture of what is being learned. At this point, that type of test reform is necessary to really understand what is being taught and learned in our K-12 classrooms.

Concluding Thoughts

It's time to tear apart the traditional way our K-12 students have been tested and look for a more targeted approach that implements technology, focuses on information gathering, and accounts for the differences between the students who take the assessments. It will take a lot of work and the initial cost outlay may be substantial, but the end result will be effective assessments that actually tell us something about the progress of individual students.

If we really want to make our public schools places that deliver the brightest minds of their generations, then we owe it to these students to make testing fair and beneficial. It should not simply be a process involving measuring sticks and statistics; assessments should give us a wider, more detailed perspective on what our students have learned so far, how they've learned it, and what their learning outlook is for the future.

References

Baker, Al. 2012. "At Top School, Cheating Voids 70 Pupils' Tests." *New York Times*, July 7. Accessed September 9, 2016. http://www.nytimes.com/2012/07/10/nyregion/70-students-at-stuyvesant-to-retake-exams-after-cheating-case.html?_r=0.

Common Core State Standards Initiative. "Read the Standards." Accessed July 17, 2013. http://www.corestandards.org/read-the-standards/.

Common Sense Media. 2009. "35% of Teens Admit to Using Cell Phones to Cheat." *Common Sense Media*. Accessed July 13, 2014. https://www.commonsensemedia.org/about-us/news/press-releases/35-of-teens-admit-to-using-cell-phones-to-cheat.

Elder, Linda, and Richard Paul. 2012. *Critical Thinking: Tools for Taking Charge of Your Learning & Your Life*. 3rd edition. Upper Saddle River, NJ: Prentice Hall.

LaBree, Shannon. 2016. "Technology and Change: School Then vs. Now." *Edmentum*. Accessed September 9, 2016. http://blog.edmentum.com/technology-change-school-then-vs-now.

Leal, Fermin. 2012. "Report: U.S. Students Lack Writing Skills." *The Orange County Register*, September 14. Accessed July 8, 2014. http://www.ocregister.com/articles/students-371409-writing-graders.html.

Nolop, Bruce. 2013. "Our College Graduates Can't Write!" *Wall Street Journal*, October 9. Accessed July 8, 2014. http://blogs.wsj.com/experts/2013/10/09/our-college-graduates-cant-write/.

Overman, Stephanie. n.d. "Fighting the Stress of Teaching to the Test: Educators Cope with Test Stress in Unique Ways." National Education Association. Accessed September 9, 2016. http://www.nea.org/tools/fighting-stress-teaching-to-Test.html.

Paul, Richard. 2004. "The State of Critical Thinking Today." *Critical Thinking*. Accessed July 25, 2014. http://www.criticalthinking.org/pages/the-state-of-critical-thinking-today/523.

Rich, Motoko. 2012. "U.S. Students Still Lag Globally in Math and Science, Tests Show." *New York Times*, December 11. Accessed July 8, 2014. http://www.nytimes.com/2012/12/11/education/us-students-still-lag-globally-in-math-and-science-tests-show.html?_r=2&.

Strauss, V. 2012. "One Teen's Standardized Testing Horror Story (And Where It Will Lead)." *Washington Post*, November 9. Accessed September 9, 2016. http://www.washingtonpost.com/blogs/answer-sheet/wp/2012/11/09/one-teens-standardized-testing-horror-story-and-where-it-will-lead/.

Wang, Yanan. 2016. "Proposed Texas Textbook Says Some Mexican Americans 'Wanted to Destroy' U.S. Society." *Washington Post*, May 24. Accessed September 9, 2016. https://www.washingtonpost.com/news/morning-mix/wp/2016/05/24/proposed-texas-textbook-says-some-mexican-americans-wanted-to-destroy-u-s-society/.

White House. n.d. "Race to the Top." Accessed September 9, 2016. https://www.whitehouse.gov/issues/education/k-12/race-to-the-top.

Black Boys in Crisis
What Can We Do?

- The school-to-prison pipeline: High school dropouts, a large percentage of whom are minorities, are at greater risk of being incarcerated.
- Why care about the school-to-prison pipeline? The costs to our society and economy are enormous.
- How to break the school-to-prison pipeline: Prevention tactics have been shown to succeed.
- Black boys aren't reading: The dismal literacy rate has a pronounced effect on the educational achievements of black boys. Intervention plans and targeted reading can help.
- Black boys and special education: Black boys are more likely than any other group to be placed in special-education classes. What are the causes, and how can we ease this burden?
- A lack of positive role models: Providing black male role models has been shown to dramatically improve student achievement.

Edmond Shoat, a Chicago high school student, dropped out just two weeks before graduation. "I was on probation. I was jobless. I didn't have nothing," Edmond says. "With only two weeks left, I just gave up on everybody. I didn't care no more. Like man, forget everybody. F everybody. I just couldn't do it no more. It was too much going on." Edmond, who had been held back a year, was nineteen at the time. By any estimate, he has had a hard life. He grew up in the Cabrini Green project, notorious for its gang violence. His uncle, who wasn't much older than he, was murdered near their apartment—Edmond heard the shots and rushed out to find his uncle dead (Arruza 2012).

Following that experience, the family tried to get themselves into a better situation. "I'd say about a month later, my whole family moved out of the projects," says Edmond. "My mom, she worked at a nursing home. And you know, sometimes she'd either quit the job or we'd have to move. We couldn't pay the rent. Or we'd find another job and move somewhere else. We did a lot of moving around" (Arruza 2012).

Edmond found himself at Senn High School, one of the worst-performing schools in an area known for terrible schools. He didn't do badly, however, and got on the football team. But one day he got into a fight, which escalated and eventually landed him in jail for a week, on a charge of illegally possessing a weapon (a pocketknife he'd forgotten about—it wasn't used in the fight). Around the same time, he became a father: his three-year-old son, Rajan, now lives with the child's mother in Atlanta (Arruza 2012).

A chemistry teacher at Senn, Antonio San Agustin, tried to help Edmond stay on track with his studies while the teen was in jail and working his way through the court system. "He was a good kid," Agustin remembers. "And he came to class, always looking to make up his assignments, because he was absent quite a bit. I didn't have problems with him making up the assignments" (Arruza 2012)

But even the intervention of concerned teachers couldn't keep Edmond in school. He flunked his first attempt at the GED and now has a low-paying job. He dreams of being able to move to be closer to his son, and of eventually becoming an actor. But the statistics are not on his side (Arruza 2012). What could have kept Edmond in school? What could have helped him succeed?

Educating Black Boys in America

When we talk about reaching students in our classrooms who come from disadvantaged backgrounds, we tend to put several groups under one umbrella. Minority students. Immigrant students. Kids from low socioeconomic households. While it's true that all of these groups of students need a different approach than their white, English-speaking, middle-class peers, our education system is not yet doing enough to address specific needs within these at-risk groups. The initiatives that help one group tremendously may not have as large a positive impact on another, and vice versa.

Black boys are a student demographic that has been, and continues to be, misunderstood in P-20 classrooms. Misbehavior, learning styles, and social skills are often misconstrued as problems by educators, when in fact black boys are simply not receiving the most effective forms of discipline, lessons, and peer-interaction opportunities. As a result, many are slipping through the proverbial cracks and not learning at their potential levels. That lack of learning leads to higher school dropout levels, higher rates of poverty, and higher incarceration rates ("Racial Disparity" n.d.).

Perhaps there is no real connection between the academic failures of black boys and incarceration/poverty, or the similar statistics associated with young Latino men. Are these young people simply bad apples, destined to fail academically and then live a life of crime? Proponents of genetic predisposition would argue that these young men never stood a chance at success and have simply accepted their lots in life (Cohen 2011).

When I hear these sorts of excuses for why we aren't best serving the black boys in our classrooms, I often think they are just too easy to be the right answers. They are all just too convenient, particularly if the people speaking them into existence come from backgrounds and experiences that are dissimilar to those typical of young black men.

Scoffing at the connection between a strong education and a life lived on the straight and narrow is an easy way to bypass the real issues in K-12 learning that actually put real barriers in place for black boys. What if the failure of black boys to succeed is really society's fault, not theirs?

While there is always a level of personal responsibility on the part of the student, I believe all of society's failures when it comes to black boys are traceable to education. Placing the blame on outside factors, such as family setup or poverty, does not actually solve the problem. Schools, particularly public ones, are great equalizers for our children and youth. When we have disadvantaged students in our midst, why aren't we employing every tactic we've got in trying to combat those detrimental outside factors? When we throw up our hands and say that black boys can't be saved, or that individual students are better off being expelled than sitting in our classrooms learning, we are really saying that we don't have any power in the lives of our students. I think most rational educators would find that notion repellent.

Consider this: Black students tend to have fewer teachers who are certified in their degree areas. A US Department of Education report found that in public high schools with at least 50 percent black students, only

75 percent of math teachers were certified, compared to 92 percent in predominantly white schools. In English, the numbers were 59 and 68 percent, respectively, and in science, they were 57 percent and 73 percent, respectively (National Center for Education Statistics, Institute of Education Sciences 2010). Numbers like these are just the tip of the iceberg when it comes to the disadvantages that take place in schools where children of color are the majority, however.

The aim of this chapter is not to wallow in pity, but rather to lead us away from the excuses that keep us from improving the public-school experiences of black boys and other at-risk groups. We must get to a place where we are so certain that change is possible that we are eager to move into action.

As an educational community, it's time to stop acting like generational poverty and crime are unrelated—that harsh discipline in schools is not related to incarceration rates. Low rates of literacy and high rates of special-education referrals among black boys aren't coincidences (National Education Association 2011). There isn't just one reason that black boys are failing on such a large scale; the factors that play into the general underachievement of the young black men in our classrooms are varied and complicated. It will take time to solve all the problems; improving the achievement of black young men in our schools won't happen overnight.

Starting from a place of understanding, grounded in facts, is a good jumping-off point. Information has a way of triggering action, which is the hope for this chapter. For every obstacle that black boys face, I will discuss practical strategies that educators can use to overcome them.

The School-to-Prison Pipeline

High school dropouts in all demographics have a higher likelihood of incarceration at some point in their lives. Sadly, over half of young black men who attend urban high schools do not earn a diploma. Of the dropouts, nearly 60 percent will go to prison at some point (Crotty 2011). In fact, the Sentencing Project projects that one in three black men will likely see the inside of a prison cell at some point in their lives ("Racial Disparity" n.d.). The connection here is not just superficial. Yes, it's fair to say that high school dropouts are more likely to commit crimes because they do not have the means to make an honest living, but I also think this connection centers on a mentality. The same black boys who believe they aren't good enough to earn the basic American right, a high school diploma, are the ones who feel they cannot make a solid contribution to society at large.

In order to delve more deeply, we need to go even further back. The decision to drop out of high school, after all, isn't reached overnight. There are many factors that play into a student's choice to not continue on to earn a high school diploma, some that are completely out of the control of the school and others that are influenced by it.

Look into the face of any kindergarten student and you'll find innocence, unquenchable curiosity, and potential. More so than in the grades that follow, kindergarten is a mixed bag of developmental, social, and academic levels. Some kids arrive with a few years of childcare and preschool under their belts, while others have never even had a book read to them. The students who arrive in these kindergarten classrooms are already products of their limited life experiences, but their public-school classrooms are intended to be equalizers. In a perfect world, what has happened outside the classroom should not be a factor in the learning environment and all students should begin with the same clean slate.

The reality, of course, is that the behavior of children is impacted by their life experiences and that behavior does impact the way a classroom functions. Kindergarten is just the first opportunity in our official public-school system for teachers to effect positive change in students who need it from a behavioral standpoint—the real work starts before that, though. The US Department of Education Office for Civil Rights reports that black students make up just 18 percent of preschoolers but account for almost half of all school suspensions. Those statistics don't improve with age. Around 5 percent of white students are suspended or expelled at some point in their K-12 careers, compared with 16 percent of black students (U.S. Department of Education Office for Civil Rights 2014).

Enter the school-to-prison pipeline, or the correlation between students who are removed (suspended or expelled) from school and those who end up in prison at some point in their lives. Students who are removed from school, either temporarily or forever, also drop out of high school at much higher rates than students who are never removed from a classroom setting.

A study published by the University of Pennsylvania reports that black students make up 39 percent of students suspended in Florida, which doesn't sound all that terrible until you consider another statistic: black students only account for 23 percent of the public-school population in

Florida (Harper n.d.). The study notes that black students are suspended and expelled more due to "unfair discipline practices."

While the numbers for the state are bad, it gets worse in Orange County in the central part of the state where Orlando is located. Though they make up just 27 percent of the county's public-school population, black students represent 51 percent of the students suspended (Postal 2015).

Eighteen percent of the nation's public-school students are black but an estimated 40 percent of students expelled from US schools are black (Stevenson 2013). This makes black students over three times more likely to face suspension or expulsion than their white peers. When you add in Latino numbers, 70 percent of all in-school arrests are black or Latino students (Stevenson 2013). Furthermore, 61 percent of the incarcerated population is black or Latino—despite the fact that these groups only represent 30 percent of the US population when combined. Nearly 68 percent of all men in federal prison have never earned a high school diploma (The Sentencing Project 2016).

Given this information, the fact that the United States has the highest incarceration rate in the world is no surprise. The road to lockup starts in the public-school systems—and it starts with unfair punishment. Over and over, statistics indicate that punishment for black boys—even for first-time offenders—in schools is harsher than for any other demographic.

Black boys taken from schools in handcuffs are not always violent, or even criminals. Increasingly, school-assigned law-enforcement officers are leading these students from their schools hallways for minor offenses, including class disruption, tardiness, and even nonviolent arguments with other students. It seems that it is easier to remove these students from class through the stigma of suspension or arrest than to look for in-school solutions.

Minnesota civil rights attorney Nekima Levy-Pounds writes, "It is a continual affront to the human dignity of black boys to be treated as second-class citizens within the public school system and made to feel as though they are not welcome in mainstream classroom settings" (Levy-Pounds 2015).

Simply put, the currently accepted way of disciplining students—primarily "zero-tolerance" policies—is doing young black boys more harm than good.

When one student is causing a classroom disruption, the traditional way to address the issue has been removal—whether the removal is for five minutes, five days, or permanently. Separating the "good" students from the "bad" has always seemed a judicious approach. If all children came from homes that implemented a cause-and-effect approach to discipline, this might be the right answer. Unfortunately, an increasing number of students come from broken homes, or homes where parents don't have the desire or time to discipline. Even the parents with the skills to discipline in this fashion may not have the time or energy, especially in a home where finances are tight. For these students, removal from education is simply another form of abandonment and entrenches the feeling that they are not good enough to learn alongside their peers.

High-profile instances of school violence in recent years have led to a higher presence of law-enforcement officers in public schools, often politely labeled as resource officers or a similarly vague term. Of course, the presence of guns and other immediately dangerous items in schools is cause for arrest, or at least temporary removal of the student, but the American Civil Liberties Union reports that children as young as five who are throwing tantrums have been removed in handcuffs by police officers (ACLU, n.d.). Rather than addressing the individual problems, it is easier for public schools to weed out troublesome students under the umbrella of protecting the greater good. Convenience trumps finding actual solutions.

The term "zero tolerance" may sound like the best way to handle all offenses in public schools, but it really does a disservice to students. Not every infraction is a clean-cut issue and not every misstep by a student is a result of direct defiance. Often students with legitimate learning disabilities or social impairment are labeled as "disruptions" and removed from classroom settings under the guise of preserving the learning experience for other, better-behaved students. There is, of course, an argument to be made for protecting straight-and-narrow students from the sins of others, but we must also consider the costs.

Educators should approach students from disadvantaged backgrounds with more understanding and fewer preconceived notions. Behavior is a choice, but for students who have never seen the right way to act modeled for them, or who are looking for that extra bit of attention in classrooms, bad behavior is an academic disadvantage. Instead of spending less time in classrooms, black boys, and especially those with minor behavioral issues, should be encouraged to participate more in the learning experience.

Why Care About the School-to-Prison Pipeline?

People who fall outside this fringe group of perceived misfits may wonder why the school-to-prison pipeline should matter to them. Outside of caring about the quality of life for other individuals, which is really something that is not teachable, the school-to-prison pipeline matters in more tangible ways. Each federal prisoner costs taxpayers $28,948 per year based on 2012 statistics, which is about $79 per day (United States Courts 2013). That's a measurable cost. What isn't measurable is the indirect impact those incarcerations have on the economy because these prisoners are not contributing to the workforce. Sure, we may pay the salary of prison employees or the CEOs of large prison privatization corporations, but we are missing out on the positive impact these prisoners could have on our economy.

This is an American problem. It hurts everyone. If we want more high school graduates, less crime, and a more robust economy, we have to stop punishing black boys with school removals or discipline effects that don't match the offense.

How to Break the School-to-Prison Pipeline

If removal and zero-tolerance policies don't help black male students in the long term, what is the best way to discipline students when they do misbehave? The answer is found long before the moment when discipline is necessary. Prevention and intervention tactics need a place in all teaching pedagogy, and those tactics must adjust for demographics and individual students. Schools need to offer robust programs for at-risk students that include mentoring from older students, after-school tutoring, and customized learning. If all of this sounds like a lot of work, that's because it is. Technology is making the customized learning portion much easier, though, and allows teachers to analyze student performance in a streamlined way long before problems arise. Teachers must approach behavioral problems in the same way they approach academic problems—with an analytical eye that looks for a solution that will benefit everyone. Notice that I didn't say the easiest or best for all the other students in class. I said the best solution for *everyone*—the teacher, the peers, and individual student. The benefits of keeping a child in class, or at least in school, far outweigh the downsides of emotionally kicking a child out of class or recommending suspension.

Educators can certainly strive to reduce suspension and expulsion rates with better intervention strategies. But what about the students who choose to walk away from their educations and drop out of high school?

In an essay entitled "A Broken Windows Approach to Education Reform," *Forbes* writer James Marshall Crotty makes a direct connection between dropout and crime rates. He argues that if educators would simply take a highly organized approach to keeping kids in school, it would make a difference in the crime statistics of the future. He says: "Instead of merely insisting on Common Core Standards of excellence, we must provide serious sticks for non-compliance. And not just docking teacher and administrative pay. The real change needs to happen on the student and parent level" (Crotty 2013).

Crotty (2013) cites the effectiveness of states that do not extend driving privileges to high school dropouts or that take away athletic activities for students who fail a class. With higher stakes associated with academic success, students will have more to lose if they walk away from their education. And the higher the education level of a student, the lower the risk of criminal activity, statistically speaking.

Students who are at risk of dropping out of high school or turning to crime need more than a good report card. They need alternative suggestions on living a life that rises above their current circumstances. For a young person to truly have a shot at an honest life, he or she has to believe in the value of an education and its impact on good citizenship. That belief system has to come from direct conversations about making smart choices with trusted adults and peers. All high school students should know how much less a dropout makes than peers with a diploma.

It's not enough to imply that dropping out of high school is a bad idea; students should have all the facts. For students who struggle socially or behaviorally in high school, schools should intervene with non-traditional options such as online courses. This is also true for students who feel the pressure to start earning a living early. The technology is already in place for all students, regardless of discipline issues or life circumstances, to earn a high school diploma. The true key to ending the school-to-prison pipeline for black boys is keeping them in classrooms instead of removing them, and getting them across the stage to receive their high school diplomas. It will take an organized shift in ideology, but it is possible, even in the current generation of students.

Black Boys Aren't Reading

Literacy is the basic building block for an academic career and the lifetime that follows it. Research shows that children who come from homes where reading was a priority, and who were read to by their parents, perform better academically throughout their lives. The National Center for Education Statistics reports that kindergarten students who are read frequently to at home are more likely to be able to count to twenty, write their names, and read. Only 53 percent of children aged three to five are read to every day by a family member, however, and that number drops significantly for families with incomes below the poverty line (National Center for Education Statistics 2000). The importance of parental influence in reading extends beyond the youngest grades.

Reading isn't important just for its own sake, though. Literacy is the foundation of all other learning endeavors. Educational Testing Services reports that students who read more in their homes perform better on math assessments (Educational Testing Service 1999). The connection between reading in early childhood and its impact on future years is clear. Since parents, grandparents, and siblings are the default role models most of the time during that vital zero-to-five age group, the responsibility to instill early literacy falls on families.

The problem is especially trenchant for black boys. Only 10 percent of eighth-grade black boys in the United States are proficient in reading. In urban areas such as Chicago and Detroit, that number is even lower (Holzman 2013). By contrast, the 2013 National Assessment of Education Progress found that 46 percent of white students are adequate readers by eighth grade (*The Nation's Report Card: A First Look* 2013). The achievement gap is startling, but the difference between the NAEP report on black students as a whole and the stats on black boys is even more troubling. This is where that important dissection between at-risk groups needs to take place. It is not simply black children in general who appear to be failing in the basics, like literacy; it is the boys.

Where does that disconnect arise? Extrapolating from the NAEP data, a brother and sister from the same household could have vastly different literacy levels, even if they come from the same environment and are read to the same amount of time (even if that amount of time is none). The blame for that difference—that gap in literacy achievement—shouldn't fall on parents. That's the fault of our schools. Literacy learning is tailored to girls. So how do we adapt it to better reach our boys—and particularly our young men of color?

Reading is only one piece of the school puzzle, of course, but it is a foundational one. If the eighth graders in our schools cannot read, how will they ever learn other subjects and earn a high school diploma? Reading scores tell us so much more than the confines of their statistics, and I believe these numbers are the key to understanding the plight of young black men in our society.

Developing Black Readers

The statistics point to a startling, yet simple, truth: black boys who cannot read are already in trouble. So if we know that black boys aren't reading at the level they should, what can we do to improve that? It starts with awareness and moves on to:

Customized Reading Plans

A large part of improving the reading rates of black boys is to provide curriculum plans that are less rigid and more nuanced. As adults, the reading materials we pick up for the pure joy of reading are as varied as we are, and it's acceptable for individuals to prefer certain genres over others. Kids don't have the same freedom. In fairness, before kids can determine what reading materials they will love, they must first have exposure to a wide variety of texts. However, as we all know, when reading is uninteresting, it's hard. Early-learning teachers, from preschool through elementary school, must have a diverse knowledge of the reading materials available for their age groups and try, try, and try again until a certain subject or genre clicks.

The idea that all kindergartners should read exactly the same things is not only flawed, it's unnecessary. Today's technology makes it simple for children to read a variety of materials that are equal in grade level, though they cover different topics. There is even educational software that creates supplemental and testing materials based on the individual pieces that children read so that teachers are not tasked with writing twenty different lesson plans based on reading preferences. Some young children love fantasy; others are more interested in the way things work, or in diverse cultures. Diversity in reading materials and the ability to choose what to read based on interests will go a long way toward pulling black boys into the literacy realm early on and keeping them there. This is true from preschool through college graduation. This strict adherence to a literary canon filled with mainly white male authors and viewpoints hurts all of our students, but particularly those of color. To instill a love for reading our students have to genuinely love what their eyes see. That view must expand to include much more diversity in options, both electronic and books in hand.

Educational leaders should ensure that the classrooms and libraries in their schools are stocked with a broad range of books, including books by authors of color and books on every conceivable subject area. Don't shy away from comic books or books on shark attacks—those are often the books that young boys devour, and can be the first step on the road to reading.

Intervention Targeting

The concept of learning everything first, and testing last, is starting to leave our classrooms—but not fast enough. Feedback throughout the learning process, and taking immediate action when students are falling behind, is a much smarter way to keep students invested in learning. A student who misses out on a learning concept will not learn at the next level, and that will continue indefinitely until remediation occurs. Teachers are on the frontlines of intervention, and parents are close behind. Parents whose own parents weren't involved in their learning pursuits may not know how to follow their kids' progress, and some may simply not care. When either scenario takes place, it falls to the teacher to step up and fill in the learning gaps.

When it comes to intervention targeting, kindergarten teachers should take entry assessments as more than a baseline number; they should see them as a call to action. Specific actionable steps should be at the disposal of the teacher so when certain weaknesses are noted, there is a plan in place that addresses them. These plans must be thorough and come with benchmarks that delve deeper than what the average and above-average students must achieve. Does this mean more work for teachers? There will be some extra upfront time and planning time, yes, which is why entire school systems must recognize the need for better reading intervention that begins on day one of kindergarten, whether that manifests itself in more teacher aides, better technology for reading customization, or more reading specialists on staff.

I'm not suggesting that teachers label and remediate every student individually; rather, that more concrete policies on how to bring students up to speed should be put in place in school districts around the country. In public schools this is especially vital. While it's true that some parents choose public schools, the majority of children attend out of default. It's not a bad thing—but parents who take the time to research and send their children to non-public options often have the time and energy to follow the academic journeys of their kids. There's a stronger chance that a child in a public school needs the extra-watchful eye of a teacher in order to reach his or her goals. That eye can't just observe; it must take what it sees and use it as a tool to strengthen academic weaknesses.

Black Boys and Special Education

Black boys are more likely than any other group to be placed in special-education classes. In fact, 80 percent of all special-education students are black or Hispanic males. Black boys account for 20 percent of US students labeled as mentally retarded, even though they represent just 9 percent of the population. On the other end of the extreme, black boys are 2.5 times less likely to be classified as "gifted and talented" even if their academic record shows that they have the potential (National Education Association 2011).

An objective analysis of these statistics would indicate that there is something genetically wrong with these young men that is causing a higher incidence of disabilities and smaller percentage of gifted individuals. Educators know better. While some of the black boys categorized as special-education students belong in that grouping, many are simply misunderstood. Those behavior issues mentioned earlier in this chapter? You'd better believe that those play a role in where these students are placed in the school hierarchy. While unpleasant behavior is certainly a symptom of some learning disabilities, such as ADHD and some degrees of autism, it isn't in and of itself a disability. A lack of understanding surrounding how black boys interact with the world, and a quick trigger when it comes to disciplinary and removal practices, is contributing to higher-than-average numbers of black boys in special-education classrooms. This is not something that any educator can sit by and let continue, for it impacts the way all students are treated in the public-school landscape.

Solving the Problem of Black Boys in Special Education

The statistics on high numbers of black and Latino boys in special-education programs is more than an interesting tidbit—it's a call to action (National Education Association 2011). What can we do to identify true learning delays and isolated behavior problems and disentangle them from disabilities?

Early Intervention

Here we are again, using the word *intervention* to identify an actionable step to improve academic success for black boys. There's a reason *intervention* is more than just a buzzword; catching developmental delays early on shows the greatest promise for improvement. This starts before kindergarten, in the Head Start programs across the country and state-run intervention initiatives, such as Florida's Early Step program. Investments in early education have shown to return as much as $17.07 to society on every dollar spent (Karoly 2005).

When black boys with obvious developmental delays do wind up in kindergarten classes, it's vital that teachers spot it. This takes specialized training that should be updated and repeated throughout a teacher's career to address the ever-shifting issues facing our youngest students. Teachers must look beyond their preconceived notions of learning disabilities to determine which students may have a shot at overcoming the hurdles and avoiding the special-education label. Rather than grouping students for life, we need to start looking at some academic and behavioral issues as temporary, and applying the resources we have at our disposal to guide students over the hurdles.

Cultural Awareness

It's vital that teachers have knowledge about the lives of students outside of their own life experiences, and an understanding of how the way their behavior is impacted by it. Students without the benefit of preschool or parents who had the time and availability to teach them literacy basics will not perform as well when they arrive in classrooms. When placed beside their peers who have had such advantages, they may even seem delayed. It's important to note, however, that the first required schooling for American children is kindergarten. There is a push for more learning a lot earlier, but from a purely legal standpoint, kids are not required to show up to learn until they are of kindergarten age (which is defined as late as seven years old in some states). The cultural expectation is that these children should already have a grasp of basic skills when they arrive, both academically and socially, but for many children, especially from poorer families, this will be the first time they've seen a classroom.

Universal preschool in states such as Florida, Illinois, and Oklahoma can help bridge that learning and socialization gap for low-income families, but once again, these programs are voluntary. It's not accurate to assume that, even in states when preschool education is affordable or free, parents are taking advantage of it. There are many factors that go into the level of education families pursue for their children before the school years officially start. Compared to their peers, this puts children with no prior classroom experience at a disadvantage. But compared to what is actually required of the students when they show up on that first day of kindergarten, these blank-slate students are exactly where they need to be from a learning perspective.

With that in mind, early-grade educators must know the difference between true special-education warning signals and a kid who just needs to catch up. There are evaluation processes in place at an administrative level, but the evaluation should start in the classroom. This isn't to say that teachers should try to champion behavior or learning issues they cannot change; rather, they should simply be aware that not all children have the advantages of an early-learning foundation. That doesn't necessarily mean that all of those children have special-education needs.

A Lack of Positive Role Models

There are plenty of black men who positively impact the young men coming up in their communities. Some are high profile, while others are local businessmen or even teachers. Because of a number of factors, though, black boys have fewer people to look up to and hold them accountable than do their white, and even other minority, peers.

School is a second home to K-12 students, and black boys don't have many role models who look the way they do. Black males make up just 2 percent of the K-12 school teacher population (Reckdahl 2015). Less than 20 percent of US teachers are not white, even though minority students combined make up a majority of K-12 students (Holland 2014). It's not that educators who are female and white can't have a positive impact on the lives of their students—they certainly can and do. However, black boys need to see adults who look like them who are high school graduates, have college degrees, are successful in the workplace, and who aren't incarcerated. If that adult also happens to be a teacher, even better. Let's look at how we can make that happen in a school environment.

Better Recruitment

If we aren't seeing enough diversity in our teaching pool, perhaps we need to try harder to bring it into the industry. This emphasis on recruitment should start even before college. Young black men of promise in middle and high school should see the field of education as a potential life path. Schools of education at colleges need to offer scholarships to recruit these men and school districts need the extra funding to attract these men when they have their degrees.

The Call Me MISTER Program was first implemented in 2000 at Clemson University in South Carolina. The program was designed to "increase the pool of available teachers from a broader, more diverse background particular among the State's lowest performing elementary schools" (Edward Waters College n.d.). In essence, the program hopes to increase the low number of minority male teachers by offering scholarships to qualified applicants.

There are other programs around the country that serve the same purpose, though not all have the significant levels of funding Call Me MISTER does. What these programs do is make the prospect of becoming a teacher both desirable and lucrative.

The message of hope for men of color is spreading, both through smaller gestures and through larger initiatives. Many of the nation's largest school districts have joined President Obama's initiative to improve the educational futures of African-American and Hispanic boys, beginning in preschool extending through high school graduation—dubbed the "My Brother's Keeper" program (White House Office of the Press Secretary 2014).

The districts, which represent around 40 percent of all African-American and Hispanic boys living below the poverty line, have committed to improving access to high-quality preschool; to tracking data on male students so educators can recognize signs of struggle as soon as possible; to increase the number of boys of color who are enrolled in gifted, honors, and advanced placement courses; to strive to reduce the number of minority boys who are suspended and expelled; and to increase graduation rates among minority males. The initiative is a five-year, $200 million plan (White House Office of the Press Secretary 2014).

In Washington, DC, Schools Chancellor Kaya Henderson announced a plan to invest $20 million to support programs for Washington, DC's men of color. This included opening an all-boys college preparatory high school in 2017 under the "Empowering Males of Color" initiative (Chandler 2015). The funding for the support programs will come from private and public sources. The DC Public Education Fund is working to raise money to support these initiatives outside the operating budget.

Henderson says that her decision to invest seriously in the needs of minority boys has everything to do with mathematics (Chandler 2015). Black and Latino boys make up 43 percent of the students enrolled in DC's public schools. Graduation rates, reading and math scores, and attendance of minority boys are all lagging in the District. By fourth grade, nearly half of the city's black and Latino male students are reading below grade level (Chandler 2015). In the District, 48 percent of black male students and 57 percent of Hispanic male students graduate in four years, compared with 66 percent of their classmates. Only about a third of black male students are proficient in reading and math, compared with nearly 66 percent of students who are not black or Latino males, according to DC CAS scores (Chandler 2015).

The push is a citywide effort led by Mayor Muriel E. Bowser, who is working to improve equity and increase opportunities for black and Latino males (Chandler 2015). The efforts also align with President Obama's work to help keep male minority students in school and out of prison.

Through this initiative, young black men are given a larger pool of support, particularly from other male minorities. It's not just individual teachers or schools that are standing up for these young men; it's entire communities. These types of programs are vital to the success of young black boys because they take a multifaceted approach to improving their outcomes.

Outreach from the Business Community

Educators alone cannot turn the tide for black boys of color. It's important that those who have been successful breaking free of poverty or incarceration turn around and inspire the next generation to do the same.

An example of this in action happened at Martin Luther King Jr. Elementary School in Hartford, Connecticut. In 2015, one hundred men of color wearing suits greeted elementary students of color on their first day of school (Velez 2015). The message these men were sending was that if you worked hard and got good grades in school, you too could someday be in a position of respect. You too could achieve the American dream.

This image contrasts with the statistics, which state that black male "students in grades K-12 were nearly 2 1/2 times as likely to be suspended from school in 2000 as white students" and that most of the nearly 2.5 million people in prisons and jails "are people of color . . . and people with low levels of educational attainment" (Thompson n.d.).

On television, in movies, and online, so many kids of color see men of color as examples of what *not* to become. The criminal on the news is all too often a man of color, and so is the high school dropout. Seeing a crowd of successful black men cheering on young students was not only heartwarming, it was inspiring. A suit represents so much more than just a tailored look. It's success; it's happiness; it's an ability to overcome; it's positive. For each kid seeing that image, it's eternal.

Concluding Thoughts

One out of three black men in America will be incarcerated in his lifetime, and more than a third of the prison population is black. But this unequal rate of discipline does not begin at adulthood; it has its roots in the schools. Federal data indicate that black students account for 15 percent of the total K-12 population but make up over one-third of those students who are suspended once from school, nearly half of students who are suspended more than once, and over one-third of students expelled. Over half of young black men who attend urban high schools do not earn a diploma. And of those dropouts, nearly 60 percent will go to prison at some point ("Racial Disparity" 2016). It should be apparent that this crisis does not just affect the African-American community: the enormous costs associated with retaining students, supporting dropouts who cannot find a job, and incarcerating colossal numbers of young men are borne by society at large.

Given the dire statistics outlined above, and the current difficulties faced by the African-American population, it would be easy to assume that educating black boys is a lost cause. This is demonstrably not the case. In fact, if one looks purely at the statistics surrounding young African-American males in education, the progress is inexorably upward. Dropout rates have been steadily decreasing. The achievement gap between blacks and whites is closing: from fifty-three points in 1970 to twenty-six points in 2004 for seventeen-year-olds (Schools Matter 2015).

It is clear that, even given the tremendous obstacles facing the black boy in education, his spirit remains unquenched: he will continue to strive for the best, and is making headway in the face of almost inconceivable historical injustices. Though we are still in crisis, there is a visible path out of the morass. In this chapter, we have examined in detail the primary obstacles that continue to stand in the way of young African-American males in education, and have looked at actionable ways to tear those down, paving the way for a future of parity and promise. With this information in hand you now have everything that you need to positively impact the lives of the black boys who are in your charge.

References

ACLU. n.d. "School-to-Prison Pipeline." Accessed September 10, 2016. https://www.aclu.org/issues/racial-justice/race-and-inequality-education/school-prison-pipeline.

Arruza, E. 2012. "High School Dropout Shares His Story." *Chicago Tonight*, September 24. Accessed September 10, 2016. http://chicagotonight.wttw. com/2012/09/24/high-school-dropout-shares-his-story.

Chandler, M. A. 2015. "D.C. Schools to Invest $20 Million in Efforts to Help Black and Latino Male Students." *Washington Post*, January 21. Accessed September 10, 2016. https://www.washingtonpost.com/local/ education/dc-schools-to-invest-20-million-in-efforts-to-help-black-and-latino-male-students/2015/01/21/27450ca8-a19d-11e4–903f-9f2faf 7cd9fe_story.html.

Cohen, Patricia. 2011. "Genetic Basis for Crime: A New Look." *New York Times*, June 20. Accessed September 10, 2016. http://www.nytimes.com/ 2011/06/20/arts/genetics-and-crime-at-institute-of-justice-confer ence.html?_r=4&pagewanted=all.

Crotty, J. M. 2013. "A Broken Windows Approach to Education Reform." *Forbes*, August 30. Accessed September 10, 2016. http://www.forbes.com/ sites/jamesmarshallcrotty/2013/08/30/a-broken-windows-ap proach-to-education-reform/#67e6d30b4855.

Crotty, J. M. 2011. "Four Things I Learned from Coaching 'Poor Black Kids.'" *Forbes*, December 16. Accessed March 1, 2016. http://www. forbes.com/sites/jamesmarshallcrotty/2011/12/16/5-things-i-learned-from-coaching-poor-black-kids/#22cdba2d42b4.

Educational Testing Service. 1999. *America's Smallest School: The Family*. Princeton, NJ.

Edward Waters College. n.d. "Call Me Mister." Accessed September 10, 2016. http://www.ewc.edu/index.php/academics/academic-programs/ elementary-education/call-me-mister-program.

Grabmeier, J. 2014. "Children with Disabilities Benefit from Classroom Inclusion." Ohio State University. Accessed September 10, 2016. https:// news.osu.edu/news/2014/07/28/children-with-disabilities-benefit-from-classroom-inclusion/.

Harper, E. J. n.d. "Disproportionate Impact of K-12 School Suspension and Expulsion on Black Students in Southern States." Center for the Study of Race and Equity in Education—Pennsylvania State University. Accessed March 1, 2016. http://www.gse.upenn.edu/equity/SouthernStates.

Holland, J. J. 2014. "Studies Highlight Teacher-Student 'Diversity Gap.'" *Boston Globe*, May 4. Accessed September 10, 2016. https://www.

bostonglobe.com/news/nation/2014/05/04/teachers-nowherenot-diverse-their-students/Wq6nM4XOyoMwlOYJLtfL3L/story.html.

Holzman, M. H. 2013. *Minority Students and Public Education: Black and American Indian Students and Public Education*. Volume 1. Briarcliff Manor, NY: Chelmsford Press.

Karoly, Lynn A. 2005. *Early Childhood Interventions: Proven Results, Future Promise*. Arlington, VA: RAND Labor and Population.

Kids Count Data Center. 2014. *Children in Single Parent Families by Race*. Baltimore, MD: Annie E. Casey Foundation.

Levy-Pounds, Nekima. 2015. "Ferguson and Minneapolis Are Closer Than We Think." *Minneapolis Star Tribune*. Retrieved from: http://www.startribune.com/nekima-levy-pounds-ferguson-and-minneapolis-are-closer-than-we-think/303713651/

National Center for Education Statistics. 2000. *Fast Facts*. Washington, DC: U.S. Department of Education.

National Center for Education Statistics. 2015. *Rates of School Crime*. Washington, DC: U.S. Department of Education.

National Center for Education Statistics, Institute of Education Sciences. 2010. "Teacher Qualifications." Accessed September 10, 2016. https://nces.ed.gov/fastfacts/display.asp?id=58.

National Education Association. 2011. "Educating Black Boys." Accessed September 10, 2016. http://www.nea.org/home/42456.htm.

The Nation's Report Card: A First Look: 2013 Mathematics and Reading. 2013. Washington, DC: Institute of Education Sciences, U.S. Department of Education.

Postal, Leslie. 2015. "Black Students Disproportionately Suspended, Expelled in Florida Schools." *Orlando Sentinel*. Accessed September 10, 2016. http://www.orlandosentinel.com/features/education/school-zone/os-black-students-florida-schools-suspensions-post.html.

Powalski, S. 2013. "Bully Proofing: Helping Children Deal with Cruel Behavior." *Mumbling Mommy*. Accessed September 10, 2016. http://www.mumblingmommy.com/2013/05/bully-proofing-helping-children-deal.html.

Reckdahl, K. 2015. "Training More Black Men to Become Teachers." *The Atlantic*, December. Accessed September 10, 2016. http://

www.theatlantic.com/education/archive/2015/12/programs-teachers-african-american-men/420306/.

Schools Matter. 2015. "When Marian Wright Edelman Forgot History." Accessed September 10, 2016. http://www.schoolsmatter.info/2015/02/when-marian-wright-edelman-forgot.html.

The Sentencing Project. n.d. "Racial Disparity." Accessed March 1, 2016. http://www.sentencingproject.org/template/page.cfm?id=122.

Stevenson, J. L. 2013. "State of Equality and Justice in America: The Presumption of Guilt." *Washington Post*, May 17. Accessed March 1, 2016. https://www.washingtonpost.com/blogs/therootdc/post/state-of-equality-and-justice-in-america-the-presumption-of-guilt/2013/05/17/49a51a42-bf07–11e2–89c9–3be8095fe767_blog.html.

Thompson, T. n.d. "Fact Sheet: Outcomes for Young, Black Men." *PBS*. Accessed September 10, 2016. http://www.pbs.org/wnet/tavissmiley/tsr/too-important-to-fail/fact-sheet-outcomes-for-young-black-men/.

United States Courts. 2013. "Supervision Costs Significantly Less than Incarceration in Federal System." Accessed September 10, 2016. http://www.uscourts.gov/news/2013/07/18/supervision-costs-significantly-less-incarceration-federal-system.

U.S. Department of Education Office for Civil Rights. 2014. *Civil Rights Data Collection—Data Snapshot: School Discipline*. Washington, DC: U.S. Department of Education.

Velez, M. 2015. "100 Black Men Wearing Suits Greeted Kids on the First Day of School for an Incredibly Vital Reason." *APlus*. Accessed September 10, 2016. http://aplus.com/a/100-men-color-greet-kids-MLK-school-first-day.

White House Office of the Press Secretary. 2014. "Fact Sheet: Opportunity for All: President Obama Launches My Brother's Keeper Initiative to Build Ladders of Opportunity for Boys and Young Men of Color." Accessed September 10, 2016. https://www.whitehouse.gov/the-press-office/2014/02/27/fact-sheet-opportunity-all-president-obama-launches-my-brother-s-keeper-.

Combating Anti-Intellectualism and Academic Disengagement

- Cultural influences and intellectualism: Academic disengagement has its roots in cultural trends.
- A history of anti-intellectualism in the United States: How we got to the current state of apathy.
- How parents contribute to anti-intellectualism: The extremes of parents who depend on technology to aid their children and helicopter parenting are having a detrimental effect.
- How K-12 schools contribute to anti-intellectualism: The undervaluing of the teaching profession is creating an atmosphere of anti-intellectualism.
- Strategies for engaging students and combating anti-intellectualism: Teachers need to stop teaching to the test, and embrace programs that work, such as STEM.

When Nijay Williams entered Tennessee State University in 2013, he had high hopes: "I wanted two degrees; that's what I saw myself doing. . . . Most of the people I graduated with are not in college, but that's what I see myself doing; I want to go to college. I just want to have a degree." Williams was the first in his family to graduate from high school: his father had dropped out in fourth grade, his mother in ninth. Going to college was an enormous leap (Riggs 2014).

The university was close to his house, so Williams lived at home and worked thirty to forty hours a week to help pay for his education. He also received a $5,000 Pell Grant and took out several federal loans. To an outside observer, Williams would appear to have done everything correctly:

with a college degree, he would boost his chances in the job market (Riggs 2014).

However, under the surface, all was not well. Williams had attended a high school that did not focus on developing intellectual capability, and though he graduated from high school with good enough grades to enter college, he was simply academically unprepared for the rigors of higher education. By the end of his first year at Tennessee State, Williams lost his Pell Grant because he failed to achieve the requisite 2.0 grade average. Without that $5,000, he was unable to pay for the next year, and he ended up dropping out (Riggs 2014).

Nijay Williams is not alone. The numbers of first-generation college graduates (those who are the first in their family to go to college) are startlingly low. In fact, according to the most recent Pell Institute fact sheet, just 11 percent of first-generation students graduate within six years of starting college (http://www.pellinstitute.org/downloads/fact_sheets-6-Year_DAR_for_Students_Post-Secondary_Institution_121411.pdf; http://www.theatlantic.com/education/archive/2014/12/the-added-pressure-faced-by-first-generation-students/384139/).

Nijay Williams and many others across the United States are able to get into college, but are simply not equipped to do college-level academic work. In January 2015, President Obama issued a directive called "America's College Promise," which would make two-year college free for all Americans (White House Office of the Press Secretary 2016). However, if students are unable to succeed in the college environment, the program will certainly fall flat. It should be noted, further, that most first-generation college students are from minority or low-income families.

A primary issue, as we will see in this chapter, is that high school education in the United States is being undermined by anti-intellectualism.

Cultural Influences and Intellectualism

Americans like to revel in their high ideals. Terms like "all men are created equal" and "life, liberty and the pursuit of happiness" make us swell with pride. The cultural ideologies of freedom of religion, a democratic government, and the ability to ascend socioeconomic classes with hard work are ingrained in American children as early as pre-K educational settings. These ideals are certainly admirable, but unfortunately they are being undermined by a trend toward anti-intellectualism. Accustomed to instant gratification through technology and a classroom culture that encourages teachers to "dumb down" lessons so all students are on the same plane, K-12 students are the product of an attention-grabbing, media-obsessed society and an educational system that tries to compete with those flashy messages. The outcome is a growing group of students who not only know much less than their ancestors did, but care very little for educational pursuits that have no effect on their day-to-day lives.

Academic disengagement does not discriminate. Researcher Laurence Steinberg found that economic status, race, and ethnicity had a negligible impact on K-12 student engagement. In *Beyond the Classroom*, Steinberg concluded that anti-intellectualism and the accompanying disinterest in educational pursuits was an epidemic across the country and that the number of students who simply did not care about what was being taught has never been higher. This trend has increased in the intervening years, resulting in students who approach educational pursuits with a feeling of entitlement based on years of low expectations in educational settings. A teacher who demands more than one in the past is resented by students, who feel they should not be asked to do so much. A course with difficult requirements is written off by students as being unfair and therefore not worth the investment of time to achieve the class standards. Though the "slacker" mentality certainly affects students in other countries, American students are the poster children for this syndrome.

The push for equality in education, starting with the youngest pre-K students, has had the result of devaluing the material. Instead of raising the standards for all children, the educational bar has been lowered under the guise of giving everyone a fair shot. Equality in educational opportunities and the demands placed on students are not directly correlated, though; the complexity of education should not suffer in order to appease the masses. Dumbing down American students is not a formula for progress.

All K-12 classrooms reflect cultural influences to some extent. This was true in the elementary classrooms of the 1950s and early 1960s, when children regularly cowered underneath their desks during mandated bomb drills. It was true when metal detectors first started appearing following high-profile incidents of school violence in the 1980s. It is true today, as students are more connected than ever through use of mobile technology in the classroom, blurring the boundaries between school hours and leisure time. In order to reach students and help them learn, schools must recognize the impact of outside forces on the learning experience (Spring 2009).

However, we should also ask the question: How much should educators work *with* cultural forces, and how much should they teach *in spite of* them? After all, cultural perceptions change and worldviews seem to be evolving more rapidly than in the past. Is anti-intellectualism actually fueled by the influence of modern society?

To truly understand the plight of anti-intellectualism and academic disengagement in contemporary K-12 classrooms, a broader view of American culture is necessary. There is no way to teach in isolation; the environments of students have always influenced how they respond to educational stimuli and educators today must take many outside factors into account when trying to teach academic engagement.

In order to understand how culture has fueled academic disengagement in K-12 classrooms, let's take a brief look at the history of anti-intellectualism in this country.

A History of Anti-Intellectualism in the United States

It is easy to blame the discontents of the digital age on anti-intellectualism, but the concept has its roots in early American history. As early as colonial times, influential men wrote about the danger of a public educated in progressive thought. The famous Puritan John Cotton spoke out against too much education, saying it made the learned "more fit to act for Satan" and therefore a danger to society (Cotton 1642).

Intellectuals in the early days of American colonialism were considered less valuable than those with measurable skills such as farming, construction, and other hands-on tasks. A person with lofty thoughts that extended beyond the practical side of life was not as suited to the physical tasks of building a new nation. Furthermore, most of the people who arrived in early America were not members of the European intelligentsia. They were working-class people who often fled their home countries in pursuit of freedom from persecution (Spring 2009).

The nineteenth century was more amenable to the intellectual mindset, but still placed an emphasis on rural competencies as opposed to intellectual pursuits. A productive person was viewed as more valuable than one impractically trained in classic literature or learning, and the "self-made man" who relished physical labor was held up as an ideal (Spring 2009).

The twentieth century saw the rise of a new species of anti-intellectualism in America, stemming from a nationalist perspective. The idea that love of country trumped all other intellectual pursuits was popularized in both world wars, and accentuated by the Communist paranoia and McCarthyism in the decades that followed. To speak out against war or show sympathy with other countries at odds with the United States was frowned upon, and sometimes condemned outright (Spring 2009).

That nationalist trend following the two world wars did evolve, as anti-war protests grew in strength during the Vietnam War. The anti-war demonstrations that surrounded the Vietnam War were counterattacked by personages such as Secretary of Defense Robert McNamara. Though he attempted to explain the rationale behind the alarming number of US casualties with intellectual reasoning, the American public saw through his attempt at toning down the realities of the war. McNamara later recognized his errors; however, immense damage had been done and the anti-intellectualist movement flourished as a result (Urban and Wagoner 2009).

The Information Age and Anti-Intellectualism

While the age of instant search and information at our fingertips has transformed every area of our lives, it also has eroded our intellectual institutions. The ubiquitous access to information presents a new challenge to intellectualism in contemporary America. Take a site such as Wikipedia, for example. While a victory for crowd-sourced knowledge that hypothetically has more than one side to every story, these internet sensations have fed the notion that all knowledge is equal. Wikipedia allows anyone, regardless of credentials, to post on its pages for the greater good of shared knowledge, and many of the users are altruistic and present sound information. However, it has also seen a spate of abuse, in which companies or personalities pay writers to create whitewashed, laudatory entries (Urban and Wagoner 2009). As any university professor knows, one of the first tasks in a first-year classroom is to wean students away from using Wikipedia as a primary source of knowledge.

Other online sites are even less transparent than Wikipedia. Businesses clamoring to improve their positions in search engine page-rank results commission contrived writing, disguised as expert information, designed to get consumers to their sites when a certain word or phrase is typed into a search bar. Customer-review sites give peers an idea of what to expect from a particular product or company, but even these idealistically balanced mediums tend to weigh heavily on the negative side; it is human nature to warn others of danger, not to assure them that the path is safe.

In attempting to place more power at the fingertips of the people, the digital age is actually distorting the reality of what is fact or fiction and taking many willing but ignorant participants along for the ride. A limitless online community misinforms on a regular basis. Even the information that is correct arrives fraught with anti-intellectual challenges. The information that was once confined to textbooks, library visits, or expensive encyclopedia sets is now just a click or tap of a touchscreen away. A child who is given everything from birth and never has to work for any of his or her possessions will inherently devalue those items. The same is true of the generations growing up with internet access.

While no one would argue for a dissolution of the convenience and knowledge that the internet has provided on a global scale, a return to solid, fact-based information is necessary to preserve intellectualism. At least some weight has to be given to information in order for the youngest learners to differentiate between well-researched, proven facts and the passionate ravings of people with no expertise or training. In order for American children to think for themselves, they need more information than what can be found in a search engine, or at least the tools to sort out that information when they see it.

How Parents Contribute to Anti-Intellectualism

Though many parents are waiting until later in life to have children and more are college educated than at any other point in the nation's history, American children consistently fall behind their peers around the globe in academic achievement. Educators have long had to struggle with the fact that students in places such as China and Finland outperform American students, particularly in areas of science and math. A 2012 report released by Harvard University's Program on Education Policy and Governance found that student peers in Brazil, Latvia, and Chile are improving their academic knowledge at a rate three times faster than American children. Students in Poland, Germany, Hong Kong, Colombia, and Portugal are improving twice as quickly as American students (Hanushek, Peterson, and Woessmann 2016). Growing up in such an educated population, American kids should be at the top of their game—if not outpacing other students in the world, they should at least show significant signs of improvement in their own classrooms. However, the Harvard report found that academic achievement in all areas of American K-12 education barely budged between the years 1995 and 2009 (Hanushek, Peterson, and Woessmann 2016).

America does not lack the resources, either in the classroom or at home, to create significant improvement. Rather, it lacks the desire to improve beyond what is needed to simply pass a class, to move to the next grade level, or to gain admittance to college. The motivation to know more than the bare minimum is missing, and that disengagement typically starts before traditional school begins.

Let's take a closer look at some of the specific ways parents contribute to attitudes of academic engagement, long before children set foot in preschool and kindergarten classrooms.

Dependence on Technology

So-called educational technology targets children from infancy and provides a convenient way for parents to feel good about using media in the early childhood years. Television programs and videos claim to be a parent's answer to "what should my baby be learning?" Since such programming is developed by experts who certainly know more than the average parent about child development, these marketing ploys are accepted. Programs for infants are promoted as safe in small doses, as long as parents watch them with their little ones and participate too. Instead of reading books together, parents put children on their laps and spend half an hour clapping along to classical music and gazing at bright, swirling colors on a screen.

This contrived form of "bonding" replaces tangible activities such as rolling around on the floor, naming objects in the home, or letting a baby turn the pages of sturdy board book. Despite the American Academy of Pediatrics' warning that children under the age of two should be exposed to *no* screen time, parents adjust the recommendation to fit their own family unit and routine (American Academy of Pediatrics 2016). The AAP warnings are for "other families" who use television or other media as a babysitter, not families that use it as a form of early education.

Once the two-year mark has passed, it seems that children face a no-holds-barred attitude when it comes to screen time. A University of Michigan study found that television viewing among young children is at an eight-year high. Children between the ages of two and five watch an average of thirty-two hours of television every week, between regular programs, videos, and programming available through gaming consoles. It is not that the television shows are necessarily harmful; in fact, the *Journal of American Medical Association* found that some educational television between the ages of three and five improves reading skills (Zimmerman 2005). Rather, it is the overuse of television and technology, and the underuse of basic learning activities such as reading a book or playing with a ball, that creates academic disengagement.

Furthermore, active technology, such as using a computer or tablet for toddler learning activities, can foster academic disengagement by making the learning process too easy. If a two-year-old thinks the answer is always a touch of a screen away, he or she won't learn to search for answers or show his or her work. What parents today view as newfangled educational improvements are actually modern conveniences that devalue the pursuit of knowledge.

The eagerness to let technology replace traditional early-childhood learning methods leads to large-scale problems, though the intent of the parents using that technology may be sound. Why not give children a head start on learning ABCs, colors, and numbers that are easily taught through repetitious technology applications? Parents are not deliberately leading their pre-K offspring down the road of academic disengagement or anti-intellectualism for life, but by allowing technology to define early childhood learning, the seeds of both problems are sown. Questions that cannot be answered within a simple application format become too difficult or too time consuming for children to try to sort out later on.

As educators, the issue of parent dependency on technology is a problem that has not yet been fully recognized. The first children with access to mobile applications from infancy are just beginning their K-12 careers and will likely see some of that technology made available in their classrooms. How will these children react when they are given a book to read, or receive a marked-up math worksheet that requires editing by hand? Will they scoff at the idea of non-digital requests, or handle them graciously as part of the learning process? As with any technological progress in classrooms, mobile technology certainly has its place, but educators (and the parents before them) should also be asking what is being replaced—and how much of K-12 learning should have a technological substitute. Dependency on technology, particularly when it pertains to educational goals, is an attitude planted by parents, often unknowingly, and contributes to academic disengagement by making learning too convenient and traditional learning pursuits too boring.

Education for Practical Reasons

Education is important to parents, but so is getting a job someday. Well-rounded approaches to education are not favored as strongly as focused learning programs that emphasize job skills and applications. Recently, academic engagement has taken a hit from those who believe that children should only go to school to learn practical things.

This is nothing new in American culture, as schools have long been viewed as vehicles for job-readiness. Naysayers believe students reading books from the traditional literary canon, whose authors are often referred to as "dead white guys," are not truly being prepared for a career or a way to make a living. They claim the works of Shakespeare or Mark Twain do not have a tangible application—unless, of course, the reader ends up a scholar of either author. Even the Common Core Standards, issued in 2013, has this phrase in its mission statement: "The standards are designed to be robust and relevant to the real world, reflecting the knowledge and skills that our young people need for success in college and careers." They also emphasize strengthening Americans' place in the "global economy" ("About the Standards" n.d.). There is no mention of intellectualism or education for knowledge's sake. The Common Core Standards target practical reasons for knowledge attained in K-12 learning, lending support to the idea that everything taught must have a real-world application.

This emphasis on practical learning furthers the stereotype that people who seek knowledge for the sake of simply knowing more are eggheads or nerds. Has poetry recitation ever landed a person a promotion? When was the last time an understanding of the satirical works of Jonathan Swift earned a sought-after raise at an annual review? People who are seen as wasting time with wisdom that they simply cannot use are considered un-American and elitist.

This push toward teaching skills, as opposed to content, has certainly been a longstanding part of American culture, but is at present fueled by the internet. Some believe that schools do not have to be places where students encounter classical works of literature or are introduced to scientific theories, because all of that information is readily available. According to those who advocate for practical learning, schools should not be about presenting as much knowledge as possible but should focus on skills not easily attained through a search engine. While it is true that a student who is savvy when it comes to attaining information will fare well in the current K-12 system and the workforce beyond, simply finding and repeating knowledge is anti-intellectual in nature. The idea that all information for practical knowledge already exists is detrimental to the teaching process.

In *The Age of American Unreason*, Susan Jacoby discusses "middlebrow" culture, which was a push in the early and mid-twentieth century for middle-class people to attain higher levels of sophistication through easily accessible literature, art, and music (Jacoby 2009). As the moniker implies, middlebrow leanings are viewed as intermediary between highbrow and lowbrow cultures.

Middlebrow pursuits, such as purchasing encyclopedias on installment plans or hanging up duplications of famous paintings by artists such as Van Gogh, were scoffed at by people who considered themselves higher class. Jacoby pokes fun at her own modest upbringing, in which her parents bought into some aspects of middlebrow culture in an effort to raise the sophistication level of her family. She remembers seeing duplications of famous artworks on her walls and listening to classical music on public-radio broadcasts (Jacoby 2009).

Where middlebrow culture was right, however, was in its intent. People without much money or means for higher levels of education took it upon themselves to broaden their worldviews with whatever resources they could afford. Parents in post–World War II America wanted their children to aspire to greater heights, and not just in the economic sense. They wanted their children to know more about the world and have high levels of intellect (Jacoby 2009). For these parents, a heightened level of critical thinking meant greater opportunity in social, economic, and intellectual standing. In other words, developed intellect came first and the practical ramifications of that way of thinking came second. There were no shortcuts to ascending classes, and knowledge was the key to making the jump.

Today's parents could take a cue from middlebrow aspirations, and so could the larger society. People like Facebook creator Mark Zuckerberg are idolized for their quick rise to wealth and, as mentioned earlier, the same is true of those with extreme athletic abilities. Yes, Zuckerberg is an innovator who is justly celebrated for his intelligence, but the emphasis on his worth in monetary terms often overshadows his actual accomplishments. Instead of a cultural acknowledgement of the way Zuckerberg used his intellect to grow an innovative idea, the belief that all it takes is "one big idea" to achieve extreme wealth and prestige is attached to the Facebook story. That theory bases its validity on luck, fate, and being in the right place at the right time. This does not create a thirst for knowledge but a desire for dollar signs (Jacoby 2009).

Society's obsession with wealth as a determiner of success has a direct impact on K-12 education. Practicality is just another way of saying "How much can I make with this knowledge?" The problem with the view of schools as factories churning out money-making robots is that it focuses more on economic impact and less on appetite for intellectual pursuits. If one generation of students is allowed to graduate from high school with only "real world" learning, the intellectual future of the nation is in peril. Thankfully, even with increasing pressure from parents and communities, educators still value at least some indirectly practical knowledge, and so K-12 students still have some exposure. Schooling for practicality is a dangerous trend, though, and one that threatens an intellectual future.

Education for Socialization

The sibling of the belief that schools should be places for practical knowledge is that they are also the primary source of socialization for youth. By their very nature, schools are places for socialization, from childcare establishments to colleges. The concept that K-12 schools should provide socialization as a *service* is flawed, however, and damages the image that academics should be paramount.

At an alarming rate, parents are voluntarily "redshirting" their kindergarten-age children, citing social concerns or, worse, the desire to have an athletic advantage in the years to come. A report from Stanford University and the University of Virginia found that as many as 5.5 percent of children delayed entering kindergarten as a result of parent preference (Bassok and

Reardon 2012). Lack of academic skills at the same level as peer students has always been a valid reason parents or educators decide to hold children back, but should factors outside of actual learning achievement also be considered?

Proponents of parental choice when it comes to kindergarten redshirting say that while academic merit can be measured, emotional impacts cannot. The separation anxiety that accompanies a child who goes to kindergarten "too early" can have a negative impact for the rest of the student's K-12 career, and beyond. In some cases, holding a child back may be valid. But by implementing widespread redshirting tactics, and packaging it as a choice for all children, academic engagement takes a hit. The perception that schools are first and foremost arenas of socialization takes priority and the idea that school is for *education* is lost.

"Helicopter Parenting" and Its Effects

The fact that parental actions in the formative years can lead to problems later on is a paradox for the current generation of parents, who collectively worry about and discuss their methods of child rearing. It is not enough to rear children safely to adulthood and earn the label of a "good" parent. A glance at any handful of parenting blogs shows the self-conscious nature of the job. Moms and dads debate the value of breastfeeding versus formula feeding, working full-time versus staying home with children (or a hybrid version), and how many extracurricular activities are healthy (and how many will ruin kids forever). Instead of parents defending their own views on parenting, there is a lot of handwringing and self-doubt that screams for reassurance in the comment sections.

Parents fret about their actions and daily choices in a way that was unheard of just ten years ago. However, in the debate over the long-term effects of wearing organic clothing or allowing children to buy school lunches, a more important talking point is being neglected: the involvement of parents in early childhood education and in the years that follow.

"Helicopter parenting" has become an epidemic in certain communities. For a number of reasons, including a series of lawsuits in the 1970s and 1980s over dangerous playground equipment and media stories of abducted children, parents in the 2000s began to hover over their children. Christine French Cully, who edits *Highlights for Children*, wrote about her own experiences as a helicopter parent. At one point, her son's kindergarten teacher wanted to carve jack-o'-lanterns with child-friendly knives. Cully, along with several other parents, was reticent to allow her son to use a knife. If it was sharp enough to cut a pumpkin, it was sharp enough to cut skin, right? But how else is a child going to learn to use a knife? And what better place to learn than in a supervised kindergarten classroom? Cully eventually allowed her son to participate in the activity. He loved it and "felt a real sense of accomplishment" once he'd carved his own jack-o'-lantern (Cully 2014).

Another moment when Cully realized she was helicopter parenting was when she was reluctant to let her son go down a tall slide, though he was desperate to try it. She actually physically held him back, but he squirmed out of her arms and dashed up the ladder before she could stop him. Of course her son was fine and, as Cully noted, "the look of joy and satisfaction on his face was unforgettable" (Cully 2014).

Cully came to her senses and eventually trained herself to allow her children to take solo flights to their grandparents' house and go on camping trips without her. As she says: "If adults are too directive and overly protective, it's harder for kids to develop curiosity, courage and confidence" (Cully 2014).

The epidemic of helicopter parenting has become a real issue once kids get to college. More and more colleges are finding that parents are accompanying their child to their first days of classes and are personally confronting professors when their child doesn't get the desired grade. Some parents even drive long distances to pick up their children's laundry! Colleges are being forced to implement "departure ceremonies" in order to get parents to leave: they corral the "Velcro parents" in a room, get them to say their good-byes, and then herd the students off to their new independent lives (Trip 2010).

This trend of paranoia among parents is dangerous in physical terms, but also in less measurable ways. Children who learn to cling to ideas without proof are less likely to seek out true answers academically. It is enough for these children to simply memorize what is placed in front of them, without any real questioning, because they have learned in their pre-K years that any idea is valid. Some parents may mistake this trait for tolerance or sensitivity, but without demanding the real truth for what they are learning, children have no ownership of knowledge.

A more direct attack on academic engagement comes from parents' attitudes toward reading and teaching basic skills at home, particularly in the earliest years of their children's lives. Teachers talk about it. Administrators talk about it. National campaigns that encourage parents to read with their young children "just twenty minutes per day" emphasize the need for parents to be on hand in early learning initiatives. But when it comes to parent-to-parent interactions, the issue is nearly nonexistent.

Parents' less-than-passionate approach to education fuels a larger national epidemic: the tendency of American adults to accept questionable theory as fact. Children who are unable to differentiate between hard scientific knowledge that has been tested and conspiratorial off-the-cuff comments from celebrities and biased sources are unlikely to make the effort to hunt down real truths in academic settings.

So far in this chapter, we have looked at outside forces that impact academic disengagement in K-12 learning. There are simply things that educators cannot control that shape the attitudes of the children who grace their classrooms. But what about the attitudes within schools that increase student indifference when it comes to the pursuit of knowledge? What do those look like?

How K-12 Schools Contribute to Anti-Intellectualism

New teachers enter the job with a certain amount of naivety. This is likely true of every profession but seems to be more common in the teaching field. Compare the attitude of a first-year teacher to one that has put in two or more decades on the job. The veteran teachers often lack enthusiasm, but if they do have a shred of excitement left, they have generally stopped voicing new ideas or looking for ways to innovate in their classrooms and schools. Some of this is the unavoidable march of time that takes its toll on every career, no matter the field. Some comes from weariness working in a job that often sees adversity from multiple sources: students, parents, administrators, and the community at large.

If you think painting teachers as martyrs is going too far, consider these facts. The National Center for Education Statistics found that teacher salaries were only 3 percent higher in the 2010–2011 school year than in 1990–1991. At the end of the 2012 school year, the number of days teachers took for stress-related time off was 10 percent higher than four years earlier. American teachers make only 67 to 72 percent of what a person with a bachelor's degree should make over the course of a career (Rampell 2012).

Unlike other professions that are able to implement measurable and reasonable benchmarks for higher compensation, teaching has too many intangibles that are not valued by the cut-and-dry American policymakers and public, who often paint teachers who demand better working conditions and pay as greedy or uncaring (Rampell 2012). Most teachers will say their gripes are not about their paychecks but about the principle. In a culture that shows appreciation through financial rewards, teachers are dramatically undervalued.

This issue is further complicated when pay-for-performance suggestions are made. Yes, educators want to earn what they are worth, but putting such rubrics in place compromises the teaching experience. It places more emphasis on what a teacher can prove on a standardized test than the way he or she influences a life for educational betterment. Performance-based incentives for educators are flawed because they turn students into assets that have an impact on the earning potential of teachers. Teachers need accountability, but how can they value the immeasurable goals that fall outside of testable material? All occupations have their own forms of review and feedback, but the constant testing culture of teaching lends itself to feelings of inadequacy and being underappreciated (Rampell 2012).

For teachers to truly lead students out of a state of academic disengagement and into a state of thirst for knowledge, they need to know that there are people who believe in what they are selling. It has always been understood that children may not naturally cling to intellectual initiatives, but if enough adults in their lives do, it can have positive results when it comes to academic engagement. It is a teacher's job to educate the students in the classroom beyond what a test says should be learned. However, without the encouragement from outside forces, that job becomes nearly impossible.

Too Many Standards, Only One Ranking Determiner

Imagine a construction worker who arrives at work to find a new set of federal regulations governing his job. He already has certain rules that he follows, and the new regulations add another layer of complication. A few months later he is handed a stricter set of rules from the state. It does not go against the federal regulations, but asks for even more from him. A few months down the road, he hears from his supervisor that the way things are run on the construction site are changing to better adapt to the needs of the clients. In addition to doing the actual work set in front of him in a timely and accurate way, the construction worker must answer to three entities with different rules—four if you count the actual clients . . . and thus the art of building something beautiful gets lost in a morass of standards.

Teaching standards are usually well-intended at their core, but can create a straightjacket situation for educators. Those who have a passion for knowledge that lies outside what will be tested face a dilemma: should they move forward with their calling and risk a dip in test scores, or should they simply go with the outline placed in front of them? Teachers are academically disengaged, in part because of standards dictation, so it makes sense that students will be too.

There are other factors that lead to teachers acting as agents of academic disengagement, some intentional and others subconscious, or at any rate out of their control. Every industry has people who arrive accidentally and then end up resenting their career paths. Teaching is no exception. There are teachers who become jaded, and it impacts the effectiveness of their instruction. Some educators arrive on the job without having read a canonical work of literature or who could not pick out the most famous pieces of world art in a lineup. There are teachers who bring their own political or religious leanings to the classroom, and those actions influence or deter students and take away from the academic experience.

The job of teachers is not to change the students they receive but to find the strengths of each one and play to them. However, this does not mean ignoring a push for intellectual pursuits just because a particular student is averse to learning. It simply means that the tactics for reaching one student may not apply to others. Despite what a standards-based teaching culture tells us, what is good for the many is *not* always good for the one.

How can students take responsibility for their own educations if their learning paths are dictated for them? How can teachers academically engage students when all that matters is the number on a standardized test or the ranking of a school? The idea that education must adapt to meet the needs of the lowest common denominator hurts all aspects of the learning process, even those considered the lowest common denominators.

Teachers have a unique calling when it comes to engaging students and imparting a love for knowledge that fosters a spirit of intellectualism. Educators must keep their jobs while reaching across the standards that divide them to pull in students who are already preprogrammed for academic indifference when they enter kindergarten classrooms.

Strategies for Engaging Students and Combating Anti-Intellectualism

What can do you do to engage students and combat anti-intellectualism in your school district? In the discussion that follows, I will outline several strategies.

Stop "Teaching to the Test"

Because of the stress and the potential ramifications (including job loss) of poor scores, teachers have begun teaching to the test. More time is spent with academically challenged students, and the amount of time spent exclusively on material covered by the test has greatly increased. Teachers sometimes change their teaching styles to accommodate content included on standardized exams. Their students can demonstrate rote knowledge but are unable to apply it or appreciate it in context. Test-score improvement could be attributed to the alteration of the teaching parameters, but this would not improve students' problem-solving abilities or critical-thinking skills.

If we really want to combat anti-intellectualism, we need to broaden the curriculum like it used to be back in the good old days. Back when we read Shakespeare and Mark Twain, and created replicas of the solar system. Back when education was fun and sparked our intellectual curiosity. If we move away from this system of continual assessment that forces educators to teach to the test, then we will usher in a love of learning, not an ability to regurgitate basic facts on a standardized exam.

You may think your hands are tied, but they are not. At the end of December 2015, President Obama signed the Every Student Succeeds Act into law (Nelson 2015). No Child Left Behind is no more.

The new bill makes major changes to federal education policy. It will change how teacher performance is evaluated. States will have the ability to individually appraise how well its teachers are doing performance wise. Another alteration under the new law will allow states "to come up with their own way to determine the quality of their local schools." This means that test scores are no longer the sole deciding factor for school performance (Nelson 2015). If your state takes advantage of this, it should also mean that you will no longer have to teach to the test, as school districts do not have to use standardized assessments to evaluate your performance. You will now be free to broaden the curriculum and not only give students the knowledge and skills that they will need to get a job, but also instill a lifelong love of learning and intellectual curiosity in them.

Adjust Your Attitudes toward STEM

In order for schools to end academic disengagement and also anti-intellectualism, they also have to change their attitude toward STEM (Science, Technology, Engineering, and Mathematics). A report released in December 2012 called *Trends in International Mathematics and Science Study* showed that just 7 percent of US students had advanced eighth-grade-level math skills, compared with 47 percent in South Korea and 48 percent in Singapore (National Education Center for Statistics n.d.). Furthermore, the United States was ranked as eleventh in fourth-grade math and ninth in eighth-grade math. American students ranked higher in reading, but still fell behind Hong Kong, Russia, and Finland.

When test results such as these are released, there is usually an initial public outcry about the slipping state of the American public in science and math. However, those voices quickly fade, and students are content to download another smartphone app that does metric conversion or even one that is advertised to complete math homework with a few taps of a touchscreen. It is easier to consume technology than to learn how to tackle the equations and other much-needed skills that would enable us to enhance and *create* technology.

The truth is that Americans have an attitude problem. This indifference toward STEM is a byproduct of academic disengagement and anti-intellectualism, fueled by the way children are taught in American K-12 schools. As interactive technology becomes commonplace in classrooms, education becomes more of a form of entertainment. Yes, educators should find innovative ways to reach students with educational messages. But there is a blurry line between creative learning and babysitting tactics to keep students from declaring that they're bored.

Are math, science, engineering, and technology topics simply too complicated for the short attention spans of today's American K-12 students? Even worse, do educators add to this problem by spending too much time trying to put on a song and dance? The answer to both of these questions is yes.

I am not blaming educators. Rather, I am pointing out that they are in a quandary made possible by an issue that, ironically, has been empowered by technology. Screen culture rules. So does an education system that favors standardized learning over intellectualism. Our educational system emphasizes fact memorization instead of placing a priority on hands-on math and science experiences. As a result, 46 percent of Americans believe that young people do not pursue math and science careers because they are "too hard." In the same Pew Research study, 20 percent of American said careers in science and math are "too boring" (Pew Research Center 2013).

So how do we change America's attitude toward STEM? We need to place a larger focus on STEM learning at a younger age. This does not just mean computers and mobile devices available in K-12 classrooms; it should include lessons on the "how" of the technology. The site code.org has basic coding activities for children as young as kindergarten, and teachers should be taking advantage of these resources. Waiting until middle or high school is simply too late to spark an interest in K-12 students in the STEM area (Lynch "Computer Science" n.d.).

Finally, special attention should be paid to getting young women interested in STEM. Research tells us that girls are just as adept as boys at learning STEM topics, but their interest tends to drop off in late elementary or middle school. Knowing this, educators should make sure girls are exposed to the same STEM learning as boys and encouraged through organizations such as Girls Who Code (Lynch "Computer Science" n.d.). It may still take a generation to get to the point where young women feel completely comfortable seeking out STEM opportunities, so in the meantime support systems need to be in place. In order to make our advice tangible, let's look at the initiatives schools are using to encourage students to pursue STEM careers before they get to college (Lynch "Computer Science" n.d.).

In Lanham, Maryland, DuVal High School is now offering its students the opportunity to take an Aerospace Engineering and Aviation Technology class (Lynch "Maryland Aerospace" n.d.). Nearly seventy students, including fifteen girls, are in the first class of the specialty program, which is part of a STEM offering to encourage more students to embrace these fields. Located just minutes from DuVal, NASA and the College Park Aviation Museum are serving as partners and working to expose students to career options they may otherwise overlook.

Segun C. Eubanks, chairman of the Prince George's County School Board, which oversees DuVal, said that the program is like other career academies that have opened across the country, part of an ongoing effort by school system to expose students to these high-demand fields and prepare them for college and their careers. He notes: "Rather than just explain to them why they need algebra skills in the ninth grade, this shows them" (Lynch "Maryland Aerospace" n.d.).

The academies began in Prince George's three years ago, and are an integral component of the county's secondary school reform. In those three years, it has opened thirty-six career-focused academies, offering twelve career options to 3,400 students who participated in the specialty programs last year.

School chief Kevin Maxwell said the program will give students a competitive edge when they apply for college, especially if they decide to pursue a career in engineering or aviation. The Aerospace Engineering Program at DuVal High School is a remarkable opportunity that will expose high school students to STEM subjects and provide hands-on learning (Lynch "Maryland Aerospace" n.d.).

The Florida Institute of Technology is also dedicated to helping K-12 students reconsider the role of science and math in their lives. It hopes to inspire students to seek out careers in science, technology, engineering, and math, and has started a poster outreach campaign to make that happen. Florida Tech's Office of Enrollment Management is sponsoring a program that has already sent 13,700 posters to teachers across the country. The posters pose one important query: "What if there were no moon?" (Florida Institute of Technology n.d.). The hypothetical question comes with many facets attached and elicits intense class discussion, mathematical calculations, and scientific thinking.

The poster is more than just a wall hanging, though. It features a lesson plan that outlines ways to use physics, math, and geology to calculate the mass of the moon. Three faculty members developed the lesson plan, which was then reviewed and refined by master teachers before it was sent out to teachers nationwide (Florida Institute of Technology n.d.).

This isn't the first time Florida Tech has reached out to teachers to help with in-classroom STEM initiatives. Other posters that have been created and distributed in previous years include "The Power of Math" (investigating the science and math behind speedboat design), "Gridiron Science" (the math and physics of football), "Science in Music" (STEM career fields used in music), and "Career Options in Sustainability" (Florida Institute of Technology n.d.).

Institutions of higher education that specialize in STEM learning, such as Florida Tech, certainly recognize that its next generation of students will need to arrive on campus with a much larger knowledge set than even a few years ago. Careers in STEM fields represented 6.2 percent of the total US workforce in May of 2014 and those numbers are predicted to grow steeply through 2020, according to the US Department of Labor (Bureau of Labor Statistics 2016). That work begins long before a college career, however, and outreach such as this poster program helps build the STEM foundation that will be needed as a college student and beyond.

We need to prioritize STEM learning. But even more than that, we need to find a way to make STEM topics more fun, accessible, and understandable to students in a global economy that prizes STEM-related contributions. This perhaps is the most promising way to combat anti-intellectualism and academic disengagement in our K-12 schools.

Concluding Thoughts

In this chapter, we have explored Hofstadter's claims from half a century ago that the democratization of schools has actually hurt intellectual growth (Hofstadter 1963). Public education, measured by initiatives such as standardized testing and Common Core, is basically democratic. But by leveling playing fields and treating all students equally, is intellectual growth being sacrificed? To put it another way, are the American virtues of equality and access to free education actually hurting the progress of intellectual thought in the nation's children?

At the beginning of this chapter, we looked at the story of Nijay Williams, who was unable to complete his first year of college because his experience in grade school did not prepare him academically for the rigors of higher education. He and others like him are the real casualties of the anti-intellectual trend in America today. Unless we can find ways to reverse the trend, more students will fall behind. And unfortunately, a large proportion of them will be first-generation students or those who come from minority and impoverished backgrounds. In this chapter, I provided you with several ways that you can counteract the current anti-intellectual trend in America. While not an exhaustive list, you can use these strategies as a starting point.

References

American Academy of Pediatrics. 2016. "Media and Children." Accessed September 10, 2016. http://www.aap.org/en-us/advocacy-and-policy/aap-health-initiatives/Pages/Media-and-Children.aspx?nfstatus=401&nftoken=00000000-0000-0000-0000-000000000000&nfstatusdescription=ERROR%3a+No+local+token.

Baby Center. 2013. "Immunizations for Children: What You Need to Know." Accessed September 10, 2016. http://www.babycenter.com/shots.

Bassok, Daphna, and Sean F. Reardon. 2012. "'Academic Redshirting' in Kindergarten: Prevalence, Patterns, and Implications." *Educational Evaluation and Policy Analysis*. Accessed September 10, 2016. doi: 10.3102/0162373713482764.

Bureau of Labor Statistics. 2016. "Occupational Employment and Wages—May 2015." Accessed September 10, 2016. http://www.bls.gov/news.release/pdf/ocwage.pdf.

Centers for Disease Control and Prevention. 2012. "Vaccine Safety." Accessed September 10, 2016. http://www.cdc.gov/vaccinesafety/vaccines/multiplevaccines.html.

Child Passenger Safety Statistics. 2005. *Seat Check*. Accessed September 10, 2016. http://www.seatcheck.org/news_fact_sheets_statistics.html.

Common Core State Standards Initiative. n.d. "About the Standards." Accessed September 10, 2016. http://www.corestandards.org/about-the-standards/.

Cotton, John. 1642. "The Powering Out of the Seven Vials." Sermon.

Cully, Christine French. 2014. "Confessions of a (Reformed) Helicopter Mom." *Huffington Post*. Accessed September 10, 2016. http://www.huffingtonpost.com/christine-french-cully/confessions-of-a-reformed-helicopter-mom_b_5563445.html.

Falco, Miriam. 2012. "CDC: U.S. Kids with Autism Up 78% in Past Decade." *CNN Health*. Accessed September 10, 2016. http://www.cnn.com/2012/03/29/health/autism.

Florida Institute of Technology. n.d. "What Were They Thinking?" Accessed September 10, 2016. http://www.fit.edu/stem-poster/.

Hanushek, Eric A., Paul E. Peterson, and Ludger Woessmann. 2012. "Achievement Growth: International and U.S. State Trends in Student Performance." Harvard Kennedy School. Accessed September 10, 2016. http://www.hks.harvard.edu/pepg/PDF/Papers/PEPG12–03_CatchingUp.pdf.

Hanushek, Eric A., Paul E. Peterson, and Ludger Woessmann. 2016. "Is the U.S. Catching Up?" *Education Next*. Accessed September 16, 2016. http://educationnext.org/is-the-us-catching-up/.

Hofstadter, Richard. 1963. *Anti-Intellectualism in American Life*. New York: Vintage Books.

Jacoby, Susan. 2009. *The Age of American Unreason*. New York: Vintage Books.

Lynch, Matthew. n.d. "Computer Science in K-12 Classrooms Needs to Catch Up." *The Edvocate*. Accessed September 10, 2016. http://www.theedadvocate.org/computer-science-in-k-12-classrooms-needs-to-catch-up/.

Lynch, Matthew. n.d. "Maryland Aerospace Engineering Program Taking Off." *The Edvocate*. Accessed September 10, 2016. http://www.theedadvocate.org/maryland-aerospace-engineering-program-taking-off/.

National Center on Education Statistics. 2012. "Teacher Trends." Accessed September 10, 2016. http://nces.ed.gov/fastfacts/display.asp?id=28.

National Center for Education Statistics. n.d. "Trends in International Mathematics and Science Study: Overview." Accessed September 10, 2016. http://nces.ed.gov/timss/.

Nelson, Libby. 2015. "How Schools Will Be Different Without No Child Left Behind." *Vox*. Accessed September 10, 2016. http://www.vox.com/2015/12/11/9889350/every-student-succeeds-act-schools.

Pew Research Center. 2013. "Public's Knowledge of Science and Technology." Accessed September 10, 2016. http://www.people-press.org/2013/04/22/publics-knowledge-of-science-and-technology/.

Rampell, Catherine. "Does It Pay to Become a Teacher?" *New York Times*, September 11, 2009. Accessed September 10, 2016. http://economix.blogs.nytimes.com/2012/09/11/does-it-pay-to-become-a-teacher/?_r=0.

Riggs, Liz. 2014. "First-Generation College-Goers: Unprepared and Behind." *The Atlantic*, December 2014. Accessed September 10, 2016. http://www.theatlantic.com/education/archive/2014/12/the-added-pressure-faced-by-first-generation-students/384139/.

Salem, Dian Abou. 2013. "Redshirting in Kindergarten Still Subject to Debate." *ABC News*. Accessed September 10, 2016. http://abcnews.go.com/Health/redshirting-kindergarten-subject debate/story?id=19253486.

Spring, J. 2009. *American Education*. 14th edition. New York: McGraw-Hill.

Trip, Gabriel. 2010. "Students, Welcome to College; Parents, Go Home." *New York Times*, August 23. Accessed September 10, 2016. http://www.nytimes.com/2010/08/23/education/23college.html?_r=0.

Trout, Paul. 1997. "Disengaged Students and the Decline of Academic Standards." *Academic Questions*. Accessed September 10, 2016. http://link.springer.com/content/pdf/10.1007%2Fs12129-997-1067-3.pdf.

Urban, W. J., and J. L. Wagoner. 2009. *American Education: A History*. New York: Routledge.

White House Office of the Press Secretary. 2015. "Fact Sheet—White House Unveils America's College Promise Proposal: Tuition-Free Community College for Responsible Students." Accessed September 16, 2016. https://www.whitehouse.gov/the-press-office/2015/01/09/fact-sheet-white-house-unveils-america-s-college-promise-proposal-tuitio.

Zimmerman, Christakis. 2005. "Children's Television Viewing and Cognitive Outcomes: A Longitudinal Analysis of National Data." *Journal of the American Medical Association*, 159, 7. Accessed September 10, 2016. http://archpedi.jamanetwork.com/article.aspx?articleid=486070.

Responding to Social Promotion and Retention

- The roots of retention: The history of the pass-fail culture in America.
- The current reality of retention and social promotion: The situation in today's public schools.
- Psychological effects: What do retention and social promotion do to the affected students and their classmates?
- The challenge of implementing and sustaining effective social promotion polices: A look at case studies in Southern California and Chicago.
- Solutions: These include multiage classrooms, recognition of multiple intelligences, and integrated tracking.

Milwaukee student Don Barry's mother was aware that her son wasn't doing well in school. "I knew he wasn't good at math," she says. "And he hated teachers asking him questions—because he didn't know stuff. He wasn't going to ask the teacher. So he was probably just doing it and doing it wrong." Following the first-semester break, the school informed Ms. Barry that her son would probably be retained that year. It wasn't a shock to her, though it was to Don. Ms. Barry says, "He thought he was like untouchable and would pass anyway—even though he wasn't doing any work" (Williams 2007).

    Don Barry was indeed retained in eighth grade. The retention, according to Ms. Barry, had dramatic consequences for her son's social life. "Don felt bad like you know some of his friends knew he was still in the same grade. He got to a point where he didn't care. He started going out a lot more, like not being at home and not even trying to do his work." Don, in fact, was being bullied by his former classmates. As Ms. Barry reports: "His friends treated him like he really wasn't nothing because they were in a higher grade because they passed. They wouldn't kick it with him like they use to and when he would asked them about work or something they would start laughing at him or look at him like he was stupid or something" (Williams 2007).

According to Ms. Barry, standardized testing was a factor in keeping him back. She says, "The WKCE [Wisconsin Knowledge and Concepts Examination] at the beginning of the year. That was a major determination whether or not he should be passed. He did not do well at all on the WKCE. And along with him not doing well during the semester—not turning in work, not on track of school work, coupled with the WKCE—he was destined to flunk" (Williams 2007).

Retaining her son, Ms. Barry says, was an unqualified disaster. "I think the main reason Don was retained was not doing his work," she notes, "but he's still not doing his work, and it seems like his attitude has gotten worse" (Williams 2007).

Don Barry's experience is, unfortunately, far from unique. Boys are at the greatest risk for failing a grade and being retained, and for social promotion, which is moving children up through the grade levels regardless of their achievement so they can remain with their peers. Being retained increases the chances that they will drop out of school and creates many other social and work-related problems (Fashola 2005).

Social Retention and Promotion: A Complex Problem

The research is clear: holding children back a grade has little effect on their academic achievement and is detrimental to their social lives (Jimerson and Kaufman 2003). Nevertheless, the US educational system retains students at astronomical rates, and this is especially true for children in impoverished settings. In fact, in urban schools in the United States, such as the one Don Barry attended, the retention rate is estimated to be almost 50 percent. Furthermore, the cost of retention is outlandish: around $20 billion each year (Williams 2007).

However, social promotion is also problematic, as it inevitably means that the promoted students will not be able to do the work unless there is extraordinary intervention (Hong and Yu 2008). This chapter will look at retention and social promotion, and at ways to get around these twin obstacles.

Public educators, students, and parents alike find retention and social promotion policies bewildering. Educators often have a difficult time understanding when and how to employ the policies, and students and parents are often confounded by the strategies. The prospect of retention sends many students into a panic or depression and their parents are generally at a loss as to how to respond. Far too often, for children in America, a state of resignation sets in once they have been retained: they accept the stigma and find it difficult to imagine a way forward through the school system.

The public-education system in America has received attention from numerous reformers throughout history. Many have worked hard to improve the effectiveness of the system, but we have still not achieved much that's conclusively better. As reformers have found, developing an effective public-education system is not without pitfalls. The biggest challenges center on vague statements of purpose, insubstantial models for classroom management and teaching, faulty assessment objectives and methods, and difficulties identifying procedures that offer optimal support to all students.

How did we get to this place? In the following section, we'll take a brief look at the history of social promotion and retention in the United States.

The Roots of Retention

The pass-fail culture in the United States has its roots in the elite nature of the educational system. At the outset, education in America was viewed as an activity reserved for the wealthy: for the children of rich landowners who did not have to work in the fields, or for the children of the upper classes in the cities. For example, in 1830, a Pennsylvania committee denounced urban public schools because they served mostly the poor and stressed only basic skills (Tyack and Cuban 1995). In the South, where the majority of African Americans initially resided, this notion was even stronger than in the North, and lingered for much longer. Additionally, the powerful landowners had no desire for the working class to gain education. It was in their best interests to keep the workers intellectually subdued so they wouldn't recognize their plight and would continue to toil on the land for meager wages.

Horace Mann's reforms, which we looked at in Chapter 1, created the basis of the public educational system we know today, and his good intentions and positive influence cannot be denied. However, the elitist nature of American education clashed with Mann's exhortations to bring everybody into the fold. Students who weren't able to compete academically dropped out almost immediately, and there were no supports in place for those who had learning disabilities or who came from disadvantaged backgrounds and lacked the educational foundation.

Schools during Mann's time were primarily one-room schoolhouses, which ideally had the effect of a Montessori system: they allowed students to proceed at their own pace and teachers could group students according to ability rather than adhere to strict age boundaries. However, as one-room schools faded in the early part of the twentieth century, to be replaced by age-graded schools with multiple classrooms and specialized teachers, the ugly specter of retention began to rear its head. The basic issue was the conundrum that continues to stymie educational professionals today: Schools are mandated by law to provide education to all students. They are also supposed to achieve a certain standard of education for those students; a standard usually gauged using tests. But what if a student is unable to achieve the correct standard? Should he or she be held back to try again? Promoted anyway? Offered remedial classes and ways to make up work? Encouraged to drop out? These issues have consumed and consternated officials for decades.

The issue of retention and social promotion came to a head in the 1980s, following the publication of *A Nation at Risk*, a report written by the National Commission on Excellence in education, which stated that the nation was in peril due to the mediocrity of its public schools. The nation, the report suggested, was at a disadvantage when competing economically with Japan and West Germany, largely due to the poor state of education. *A Nation at Risk* called for reforms that would increase academic standards, improve teacher quality, and reform the curriculum (Spring 1994). Education based on standards of what all children should know and be able to do would, critics argued, reduce the practice of social promotion that contributed to the poor quality of education in the nation.

A Nation at Risk caught the attention of the American public, and by the mid-1980s most Americans believed that promotion should be based on students' mastery of grade-appropriate content and knowledge (Frey 2005). By 1998, the Clinton Administration was overtly calling for the end to social promotion (U.S. Department of Education n.d.). In the era of No Child Left Behind that followed, many states passed legislation that explicitly prohibited promotion of children who did not reach specific levels of performance on state-mandated assessments.

Retention and Social Promotion: The Reality

Though retention might seem a rational solution to the problems our education system faces, and though some studies seem to show that retention can have positive effects in the short term, it does not appear to work as well as promotion. Sociologist Robert M. Hauser says that the costs of repeating a grade are enormous and having older students in a grade often creates serious management problems. He also notes that retention has no educational benefits (Hauser 1999). Retention has a clear effect on dropout rate. Study after study has shown that students who are held back a grade are more likely to drop out. The study controlled for a number of factors, including program participation, school moves, social background, and special-education placement. A more comprehensive study by Anderson that controlled for sex, race, social background, cognitive ability, and many other factors demonstrated that students who repeated a grade were 70 percent more likely to drop out of high school (Hauser 1999).

Educational authorities have developed a number of tools to try to combat the differences in academic achievement. These include extended kindergarten, special-education services, and academic tracking, along with retention and promotion. However, because the achievement spread is so vast within age cohorts, this can lead to massive strains on teachers, who must juggle advanced children and low-performing children in the same classroom. Finding common ground for a lecture or activity can be difficult and one group is occasionally left floundering.

Psychological Effects

In the media, educational settings, and political commentary, the reasons for retention are often reduced to over-simplified clichés: "poverty," "single mother," and so on. To counter this, and to determine more precisely the factors that go into retention, as well as the long-term results of retaining students, Jessica Fanguy and Richard D. Mathis did an in-depth investigation into eight students who had undergone retention. Fanguy and Mathis were aware that psychosocial delays that lead retained students to drop out are likely to be long lasting, and in many cases permanent. They were interested in the underlying causes of retention and wanted to get beneath "the tip of the psychosocial iceberg" (Fanguy and Mathis 2012).

Fanguy and Mathis looked at eight students who had been retained in eighth grade: five white and three black; five boys and three girls. All except one were middle class; the remaining student was in a lower income bracket. In a series of interviews with the students and their parents, Fanguy and Mathis pulled out a number of factors that led to their retention. Three of the students cited environmental factors: One had been sick for a portion of the year, one's mother had been sick, and one lived in a "bad" neighborhood, with ongoing struggles due to drug transactions and the accompanying violence. Other issues included poor behavior patterns and lack of preparedness (Fanguy and Mathis 2012).

Three of the students noted that severe apathy set in after they were retained. For two of these, the apathy was directly related to an inability to perform the work. Their hopelessness in the face of difficult assignments led them to cut up inside and outside of class. Several children expressed extreme distress after they found out they had been retained. One said that she "cried and cried and cried." Others noted that they became angry and withdrawn (Fanguy and Mathis 2012).

Two students, Lisa and Beth, reported a heartbreaking sense of loss after all her friends had moved on. Beth was in tears when she recalled that her best friend moved to eighth grade and that the friendship had been severed (Fanguy and Mathis 2012).

As was the case with Don Barry, five of the eight students experienced teasing by peers. They mentioned being called names like "stupid" and "dumb." Two of the male students in the study got into fights as a result of the teasing. It is important to note that only two of the parents mentioned being aware that their students were being bullied in this way (Fanguy and Mathis 2012).

In their study, Fanguy and Mathis report the student feedback directly and clearly demonstrate the prominence of psychosocial issues that are due to the retention itself (Fanguy and Mathis 2012).

The primarily negative reaction on the part of the students suggests that retention had a strong and detrimental impact on self-esteem. There was one retained student who did not appear to react negatively to the news, but the parent report indicated that behavior caused retention in the sixth and seventh grades, with peer-pressure-influenced behaviors as well as disruptive behavior being factors (Fanguy and Mathis 2012).

Fanguy and Mathis also touched on the long-term impact of retention. Several of the students interviewed implied that they had undergone what they considered to be a life-changing experience. Others indicated they had experienced a dramatic increase in stress and an even more pronounced dislike of school. One student had received a diagnosis of Attention Deficit Disorder (ADD) subsequent to the retention. This instance indicates that the education system sometimes uses student retention as an intervention strategy before identification of a learning disability (Fanguy and Mathis 2012).

An assessment was made of low self-esteem signals for participating students in the Fanguy and Mathis study. Five of the eight student participants and five of the eight sets of parents commented that low self-esteem was an issue following the retention. One student's father specifically indicated that he felt his child had low self-esteem and another parent indicated that their child clearly "felt bad about herself largely as a result of their retention experience" (Fanguy and Mathis 2012). Two parents also reported that their children were giving up too easily and not believing in themselves, especially at school, in academic areas. One of the parents described how their child had called herself "stupid," and one of the students indicated that they were aware that they did not set high goals because they felt they could not achieve them (Fanguy and Mathis 2012).

The researchers came to the conclusion that the students might well have had fewer self-esteem issues (and a greater inclination to set challenging goals) if they had not experienced retention and if it had not proved such a negative experience (Fanguy and Mathis 2012).

Several of the students said that the teachers had victimized them, adding to the feelings of failure but also making the students angry. These students all expressed their anger at having had to repeat a year. One student described dropping out of school to escape the anger and sense of failure, as well as the victimization by teachers (Fanguy and Mathis 2012).

According to Fanguy and Mathis, only two of the students interviewed demonstrated any sign of positive self-concept. They were the only ones who described themselves in a positive light and felt optimistic about their abilities. These descriptions were supported by their parents (Fanguy and Mathis 2012).

Like other studies that have assessed retention among students, the Fanguy and Mathis study clearly demonstrated that retention is extremely destructive to a student's development on many fronts. Although not all retained students are likely to experience such debilitating self-esteem issues, anger at retention, or victimization as the students in the study we looked at above, the findings suggest that a range of problems are at work, and often leave students with a sense of failure.

Socially promoted students experienced similar problems, including poor self-esteem, poor sense of self-worth, issues with peers, anger and resentment toward teachers and school administrators, and general apathy toward school. In fact, some studies suggest that peer isolation or bullying is sometimes even more extreme for socially promoted students than for those who are retained.

Prominent developmental psychologist Erik Erikson examined identity development, and his research, which has ready application to retention and social promotion policies, sheds considerable light on these issues. Erikson specifically noted that having a high level of self-esteem was critical to identity development in adolescents. Adolescents, when they feel good about themselves, develop a positive identity, while those who do not feel good about themselves tend to struggle with their identity and can develop maladaptive or dysfunctional behaviors (Erikson 1968).

As Fanguy and Mathis point out, Erikson's theory about identity development focuses on individual psychological development, including how it pertains to adolescent life, and isolates social components of development that include family, school, and peers (Fanguy and Mathis 2012).

In their study, Fanguy and Mathis applied this theory to demonstrate the most damaging psychosocial fallout in grade-retained students.

In student and parent interviews, Fanguy and Mathis noted that the most common causes for retention were environmental stressors, apathy toward school, insufficient preparation for the following grade level, and poor behavior patterns. These were the causes that the interview subjects—both students and parents—identified as those who had led to the retention. Whether these were in fact the actual causes, and whether or not they might have been something more abstract, like the quality of teaching or the nature of the testing, presumably could not be so easily gauged from a student or parent perspective. We have to allow for who was actually assessing the cause and what their perspective was in the first place (Fanguy and Mathis 2012).

The Challenge of Implementing and Sustaining Effective Social Promotion Polices: The Long Beach Preparatory Academy Case

After a year of exposure to material scheduled for a certain grade level, our current education system demands that children either meet the material-based learning criteria (i.e., they memorize the scheduled material for the grade and demonstrate the memorized knowledge) or face one of two options: retention or social promotion. Let's look at how this plays out in a real-world example.

Long Beach Preparatory Academy in the Long Beach school district in Southern California had been hurriedly cobbled together from prefab structures in about five months. It was in a difficult neighborhood, and the school district had recently decided that social promotion, which moves students up based on age rather than test scores, had to go. Unlike other schools in the area, Long Beach Prep had plenty of money, sieved from budget reserves. They had manageable classrooms of twenty kids or fewer. They had ninety-minute classes, rather than the standard forty. The district would spend $6,300 per pupil to educate the students. (Note that this is just shy of the national average—California has had longstanding educational budget woes.) The principal, Miguel Lopes, even had the funds to hire a dean of discipline to keep the kids in line (Hubler 1998).

Adrian Chavez, his hair bleached blond from long afternoons at the shore, had been told by a teacher that he was "wasting taxpayers' money"—and it could be argued that he was. He and many other students were getting terrible grades. His classmate Brandon Perkins, an inherently bright student, had turned in a dire report card at the end of the previous year and, according to his mother, had "the attitude to go with it." Clearly the school needed to pull itself together (Hubler 1998).

The district-level abolishment of social promotion, which in the case of Long Beach Prep meant that any eighth-grader with two F's on his or her report card would be held back, had a dramatic effect on the school.

Four hundred and twenty-five students flunked, possibly the largest group in any school in recent Californian history. By the end of the year, only 292 students remained at the school (Hubler 1998).

But in the meantime, something extraordinary happened. Of those remaining students, just a handful failed to pass. Adrian Chavez was finally free to dream about becoming a boat captain, and was engaging with his teachers for the first time. Brandon Perkins' mother was astonished by his "complete turnaround" (Hubler 1998).

In the case of Long Beach Prep, cutting back on social promotion clearly created better results for the students who remained. However, what about the hundreds of kids who were expelled or sent elsewhere? Is abolishing social promotion the best way to go for everyone in the community?

Social promotion is the option that allows otherwise "failing" children to move on to the next grade level. They move on even though they have not mastered everything required, and they may even have other identified issues with skills-based learning (Rose and Schmike 2012).

Retention puts a child back a year, determining that the student should remain in a specific age-grade level if he or she has not mastered the appropriate knowledge or skills to graduate to the next level (National Association of School Psychologists 2011). The positive angle is that it allows students to take additional time to master materials that they have struggled with.

The question of whether social promotion or retention is best, or whether one is more appropriate than the other, continues to be central to the educational challenges of this country. In most school districts, the more overt practices of social promotion appear to be in decline. However, although retention is emerging as a preferred policy, many districts still rely heavily on social promotion.

The Challenge of Implementing and Sustaining Effective Retention Polices: The Chicago Case

In theory, the goal of retention polices is to ensure that students who move to the next level of learning have mastered the required knowledge and skills. The accompanying exemptions and alternative paths raise the question: Do retention and the various related supported elements actually thwart social promotion?

The problem is simple: some children may progress from grade to grade without reaching state-required benchmarks. Most states and school districts worry about the number of students who are retained without alternate avenues for promotion being made available. The general consensus, spoken or not, is that retention actually does very little to solve the underlying problem.

The retention policy path in the city of Chicago provides an overt example of the challenges associated with implementation of retention polices, and how social promotion can creep into well-intended policies meant to discontinue the practice.

Initiated in 1996, the CPS policy required students in the third, sixth, and eighth grades to reach specified scores on standardized tests for reading and mathematics, or face retention. The policy also included a summer school attendance requirement for students—the top method for avoiding retention and a transition program designed to improve reading skills of eighth grade students.

The goal was to ensure that when they entered high school, students would be able to read high-school-level textbooks. The Clinton Administration praised the policy as an effective strategy for ending social promotion. By 2011, the retention rate had shrunk from 15 percent (at the time the policy was initiated) to 4 percent (Rose and Schmike 2012).

The reduction in retention rates has reportedly not been the result of improved achievement among students, however. Both implementation and structural components of the policy have weakened over the years, which in effect compromised the policy's original intent. Apparently, CPS did not have effective means to enforce consequences for children who were not meeting promotion requirements. Students who were required to pass summer school to avoid retention were allowed to enter the next-highest grade without having to attend summer classes. High school freshmen were required to pass all freshman-level classes, however, and to achieve certain scores on standardized tests, or attend summer school to escape retention. Following later adjustments, all students who did not meet the freshman promotion requirements after their summer school attendance went into a class for failing students when they returned to school in the fall (National Association of School Psychologists 2011).

Given that summer school was an instrumental component of the CPS's policy, there was concern that if too many students were scheduled for retention, the number of summer school slots would be insufficient to handle the volume of students required to attend. The number of students performing below grade level was already substantial at the inception of the policy. Setting unattainable expectations for performance on standardized tests would simply result in an imbalance in the number of students required to attend summer school and slots available to accommodate them. Ultimately, the CPS made it easier for students to avoid retention despite poor academic performance. Achievement test scores needed for promotion were lowered so that more students were eligible for promotion (Powell 2010).

In retrospect, some administrators determined that the use of standardized tests to determine promotion was problematic. The use of standardized tests, in fact, resulted in a narrowing of the curriculum so that there would be alignment between the test administered and the curriculum taught. Students would actually learn less, but more would be able to reach required scores for promotion. This is, of course, the problem at the heart of the "teach to the test" conundrum (Powell 2010).

In the end, summer school and other interventions outlined in the CPS retention policy proved insufficient to support the number of children affected—which was inevitable, based on early number projections. Disaster followed, exacerbated by budget cuts that reduced the impact of the policy even further. As a result of the CPS budget cuts, summer schools were in session for fewer days. Summer-school class sizes also increased, undermining the potential for teachers to give proper attention to students. Budget cuts also meant a redistribution of funds initially slated to add additional teachers to schools with high numbers of retained students. Various tutoring programs were either cut or discontinued through the CPS process.

As is the case with many retention policies today, educators went ahead and promoted students if the alternative was retention for more than one year. The CPS policy allowed students to appeal retention if they were retained twice during a three-year period (Garland 2010).

Social promotion was not the primary problem facing CPS, however. Replacing social promotion with retention did not address the paramount and critical objective of the system, which was to increase learning among more students. Instead, the CPS retention initiative is a good example of noble intentions gone awry.

As a standalone policy, retention has few advantages over social promotion, and the advantages it does have are often short-lived. This is especially true in the context of high-stakes tests, when these were the primary determining factor for retention.

Since most testing begins in third grade, we have to keep in mind that there is a missed opportunity for early identification of children with learning issues. In Chicago, as in every other part of the country, retention is not effective in increasing learning if the ability is absent or other outside factors strongly impact the individual student's learning potential.

The research and anecdotal evidence all point to the same conclusion: retention is a disaster, and social promotion is not much better. In the next section, we'll look at ways of surmounting these obstacles.

Solutions

There are two keys to overcoming the issues surrounding retention and social promotion. The first is that the buckles that currently confine students must be loosened. Within the present system, a student who fails on a series of standardized tests will generally fail the grade, leading to either retention or dropout. As we have seen in this chapter, retention is a train wreck. It does not tend to boost the student's academic achievement, and if it does, the improvement is short-lived. Furthermore, it has grave and long-lasting psychological effects, as we saw in the Fanguy and Mathis study. Retention should be used as a tool only in the direst situations, and then only in the first three grades. In order to reduce retention, social promotion is necessary. However, social promotion cannot be a simple shove up the ladder. There must be a looser interpretation of grade boundaries, and less reliance on testing, in order to allow students to breathe within the classroom environment.

The second key is support. One of the fundamental supports is mentorship. All children who are socially promoted should be offered the chance to have a mentor, either one from within the school or from the community. There should also be profound, meaningful support within the school, from teachers and trained staff.

Multiage Classrooms

In Horace Mann's time, as we saw, one-room schoolhouses were the norm. These smaller, deeper units allowed students of similar ability to come together, regardless of age group. Prominent educationalist Marie

Montessori codified this idea: she advocated for more loosely organized classrooms than were usual in her time, allowing students to mingle and to move around the classroom freely. In "Montessori method" schools, multiage classrooms are especially employed in the ages three to six cohort, though many schools widen those parameters. Because the students are encouraged to learn through interaction with materials and concepts, and can proceed at their own pace, Montessori classrooms usually end up with students at many different levels. This is accepted within the Montessori system, and there are structures in place to deal with the discrepancies. Note the difference between this system and the one currently in use in US public education, where every student is expected to fit into a single mold and proceed at the same pace.

Multiage classrooms, some based on Montessori's ideas, have been used with success in public schools across the United States. For example, the *Kentucky Education Reform Act* of 1990 (KERA, House Bill 940) sought to introduce multiage classrooms in public schools across the state of Kentucky. Significant changes to the curriculum outlined in the KERA targeted the reconstruction of primary schools, especially kindergarten to third grade. Standardized testing was to be implemented throughout the state. At the same time, though, the KERA recommended ending kindergarten to third grade and replacing them with a "primary school program" that would include "multi-age and multi-ability classrooms," eliminating or at least reducing the separation of students by grade (Hoyt n.d.).

In line with the different demands of a multiage and multi-ability classroom, the KERA also outlined new and expanded requirements for curriculum content and assessment. In particular, the act outlined the need for a "performance-based" approach, with students creating a portfolio of writing and mathematics work in the fourth grade (writing only), eighth grade, and twelfth grade. Qualitative assessments, including written reports assessing students' performance, were to replace the traditional letter-grade system (Hoyt n.d.).

Further legislation passed in 1992 outlined specific attributes to be included in each primary program. The seven elements were (1) developmentally appropriate educational practices, (2) multiage and multi-ability classrooms, (3) continuous progress, (4) authentic assessment, (5) qualitative reporting methods, (6) professional teamwork, and (7) positive parent involvement. The change was modified in 1996 to allow schools greater freedom to structure programs (Hoyt n.d.).

According to the Kentucky Demographic Survey of the Primary Program used to evaluate the primary program between 2001 and 2007, the multiage program dramatically improved the academic performance of students. It also improved parents' involvement in the education of children (Hoyt n.d.).

Kentucky was not the only state to start using a multiage program. In 1994, the Michigan State Board of Education announced that it was going to establish non-graded continuous-progress programs for students in multiage classrooms (Song, Spradlin, and Plucker 2009).

Multiage classrooms were very successful in Michigan for a period beginning in 1995, when the state's department of education estimated that one in five districts was implementing multiage settings. Within three years, by 1998, more than half of Michigan's school districts had begun or were expanding their multiage models (Fox 1998). The approach was dropped in 1999, however, because funding was cut off. The following year, the Michigan Department of Education would also halt the initiative and withdraw support for multiage grouping, despite evidence that the approach helped students make progress. The key reason for the discontinuation, according to the state board of education, was the incompatibility of multiage classrooms with the grade-level content and annual testing (Song, Spradlin, and Plucker 2009).

Multiage classrooms allow students of all academic abilities to flourish and feel comfortable. However, as we saw above, implementation has been stymied by the culture of testing and federal edicts. Multiage classrooms "loosen the buckle" and should be promoted at a national level to combat retention and social promotion. I recommend that multiage classrooms should be ubiquitous through at least third grade, and ideally through sixth grade.

Broadening the Definitions

Our current testing system is obsessed with students' language and mathematical ability, and thus teachers focus on those areas. In fact, in many public schools across the country, subjects such as music, art, and physical education are not offered unless parent groups can gather the funds for them.

Developmental psychologist and educational researcher Howard Gardner, currently at Harvard, moved beyond the traditional language-and-math intelligence categories, suggesting that there are many more, all equally valuable. Gardner's categories are:

1 Verbal-linguistic intelligence
2 Logical-mathematical intelligence
3 Spatial-visual intelligence (artistic and engineering intelligence)
4 Bodily-kinesthetic intelligence
5 Musical intelligence
6 Interpersonal intelligence (ability to detect the moods and desires of others)
7 Intrapersonal intelligence (ability to be self-aware)
8 Naturalist intelligence (ability to recognize and categorize plants, animals, and other elements of nature)
9 Existential intelligence (ability to tackle deep questions about human existence)

(Northern Illinois University Faculty Development and Instructional Center n.d.).

Gardner's ideas have been successfully used in both private and public schools across the country. For example, at the high-performing Howard Gardner Multiple Intelligences Charter School in Scranton, Pennsylvania, and the Howard Gardner Community School in Chula Vista, California, students have a much broader educational experience than at traditional public schools. As the Chula Vista school says in its philosophical statement, its "project-based curriculum integrates creative problem solving into every segment of the curriculum" (Howard Gardner School n.d.). Though students at schools based on Gardner's ideas take the state tests, staff do not "teach to the test." Rather, they aim to give the students a well-rounded education, which incidentally provides them with the skills they require to pass the tests.

Schools based on the multiple-intelligences concept are so successful that I advocate for an expanded use of Gardner's ideas. We should incorporate the multiple intelligences idea not only in our curriculum, but in testing as well. This will allow students who may have, say, pronounced artistic ability but who do poorly in math to progress without hiccup. From my experience in the classroom, I can attest that students who have extremely focused abilities such as this are common. However, testing often destroys their morale: they feel they are stupid because they don't have the same skill set as higher performing children. Students who demonstrate Gardner's intelligences outside of language and math skills should be celebrated and their unique gifts nurtured.

Integrated Tracking

Currently, tracking tends to be a hit-or-miss tool. It is based on IQ tests, other tests that vary from system to system, and, occasionally, the whim of the teacher or administrator. When used effectively, however, tracking can be a very powerful tool. It offers some students more time with a subject area. For example, students who require more help in math may take it for two periods a day rather than the ordinary single period. It also offers students support in the areas where they need it. However, there is inevitable stigma associated with tracking. Here, for example, is a quote from a teacher whose school uses the tracking system: "The Regents kids of today are just a touch above our general level kids of a decade ago. Then I have the other kids who are nice kids and get decent grades, but are WAY behind the top kids. Gads, I love my period 1 and 4 honors chem classes!!!! They are some of the best kids I have ever had the honor of teaching" (Burris and Garrity 2008). Note the language used in the quote: "Regents," "general level," "top kids," "honors," and "best kids." If the teachers are adhering to this type of stratified language, one can only imagine what is used on the playground. Furthermore, it is clear where the teacher is inclined to put her emphasis: precisely on the group that needs it least. As Carol Burtis and Delia Garrity say in their book *Detracking for Excellence and Equity*, when

> observed differences are reinforced by track placement and grouping practices, and children then internalize those differences, learning opportunities become limited for all but the elite student. The talents of late bloomers go undiscovered, and the rewards of hard work and diligent study are never realized.
>
> (Burris and Garrity 2008)

Burtis and Garrity note that, though schools indicate that it is technically possible for students to move up through the tracking levels, this is in fact extremely rare. However, moving down, from a medium to a lower level, say, is very common. In other words, tracking tends to have a negative rather than a positive effect, and one suspects it is also used as a tool to control behavior: a smart student who cuts up may be more likely to be sent down (Burris and Garrity 2008).

We can take our cue from Finland, which has one of the highest reading levels among children in the world. Finland realized in the 1990s that the tracking system in the younger grades was not working. It abolished "ability grouping" in 1985 and included special education as part of the regular classroom (Coughlan 2004).

The Finnish model, and the model advocated by Burtis and Garrity, is what I would term "integrated tracking." This method keeps many of the tools of tracking, such as longer periods on certain subjects and support for students with differing abilities, but includes them within the traditional classroom. It requires teacher training and excellent staff support, but it is highly effective.

Concluding Thoughts

Retention, combined with standardized testing and rigid grade structures, amounts to a wall erected in front of children in this country. Because the wall is so high and because, in economically deprived situations, most of the children they know have not been able to surmount it, they cannot see a future beyond the wall. So they go sideways or backward, slipping into crime or trying to make ends meet with low-paying fast-food jobs or just giving up altogether.

The solutions we looked at in this chapter can help to dismantle that wall. By implementing multiage classrooms across the nation, pulling back from the focus on language skills and reading to incorporate other "intelligences," and emulating the Finnish system of heterogeneous classrooms with strong support for low-performing students, we can enable disadvantaged children to glimpse a future in education—a future that could lead them to graduate from high school, and then college, and finally enable them to land jobs that will allow them to support themselves and their family with dignity.

References

Burris, C. C., and D. T. Garrity. 2008. *Detracking for Excellence and Equity*. Alexandria, VA: Association for Supervision and Curriculum Development.

Coughlan, S. 2004. "Education Key to Economic Survival." *BBC News*. Accessed September 12, 2016. http://news.bbc.co.uk/2/hi/uk_news/education/4031805.stm.

Erikson, Erik H. 1968. *Identity, Youth, and Crisis*. New York: W.W. Norton.

Fanguy, J., and R. D. Mathis. 2012. "Psychosocial Fallout from Grade Retention: Implications for Educators." *Delta Journal of Education*, 2(2), 2.

Fashola, O. S. 2005. *Educating African American Males: Voices from the Field*. Thousand Oaks, CA: Corwin Press.

Fox, C. L. 1998. *The Michigan Multiage Continuous Progress Model*. Michigan Department of Education. Accessed September 12, 2016. http://eric.ed.gov/ERICWebPortal/custom/port-lets/recordDetails/detailm¬ini.jsp?_nfpb=true&_&ERICExtSearch_Search Value_0=ED425524&ERICExtSearch_SearchT ype_0=no&accno=ED425524.

Frey, Nancy. 2005. *Remedial and Special Education* 26(6), 332–346. First published August 18, 2016.

Garland, Sarah. 2010. "Repeat Performance." *The American Prospect*. Accessed September 12, 2016. http://prospect.org/article/repeat-performance-0.

Hauser, Robert M. 1999. *Should We End Social Promotion? Truth and Consequences*. Center for Demography and Ecology. The University of Wisconsin-Madison Rev. Accessed September 12, 2016. https://www.ssc.wisc.edu/cde/cdewp/99–06.pdf.

Hong, G., and B. Yu. 2008. "Effects of Kindergarten Retention on Children's Social-Emotional Development: An Application of Propensity Score Method to Multivariate Multi-Level Data." *Special Section on New Methods in Developmental Psychology*, 44(2), 407–421.

Howard Gardner School. n.d. "Our Philosophy and Curriculum." Accessed September 12, 2016. http://howardgardnerschool.com/about/philosophy-curriculum/.

Hoyt, W. H. n.d. *An Evaluation of the Kentucky Education Reform Act*. University of Kentucky. Accessed September 12, 2016. http://cber.uky.edu/Downloads/kentucky_education_reform_act.htm.

Hubler, S. 1998. "Snatching Victory from the Jaws of Social Promotion." *Los Angeles Times*, June 4. Accessed September 12, 2016. http://articles.latimes.com/1998/jun/04/local/me-56499.

Jimerson, S. R., and A. M. Kaufman. 2003. "Reading, Writing, and Retention: A Primer on Grade Retention Research." *Reading Teacher*, 56, 7. Accessed September 14, 2016. http://www.childtrends.org/?indicators=children-who-repeated-a-grade#_edn1.

National Association of School Psychologists. 2011. "Grade Retention and Social Promotion." *White Paper*. Bethesda, Maryland.

Northern Illinois University Faculty Development and Instructional Center. n.d. "Howard Gardner's Theory of Multiple Intelligences." Accessed September 12, 2016. http://www.niu.edu/facdev/resources/guide/learning/howard_gardner_theory_multiple_intelligences.pdf.

Powell, Pamela. 2010. "A Perilous Policy Path: Grade Retention in the Age of NCLB." *eJournal of Educational Policy*. Accessed September 12, 2016. https://www4.nau.edu/cee/jep/journals.aspx?id=326.

Rose, Stephanie, and Karen Schmike. 2012. *Third Grade Literacy Policies: Identification, Intervention, Retention*. Denver, CO: Education Commission of the States.

Song, R., T. E. Spradlin, and J. A. Plucker. 2009. "Advantages and Disadvantages of Multiage Classrooms in the Era of the NCLB Accountability." *Education Policy Brief*, 7(1), Winter, 1–8.

Spring, J. 1994. *The American School 1642–1992*. New York: McGraw-Hill.

Tyack, D., and L. Cuban. 1995. *Tinkering Toward Utopia*. Cambridge, MA: Harvard University Press.

U.S. Department of Education. n.d. "Taking Responsibility for Ending Social Promotion: A Guide for Educators and State and Local Leaders." Accessed September 12, 2016. http://www2.ed.gov/PDFDocs/socialprom.pdf.

Williams, Darrell L. 2007. "Perspectives of Urban Parents towards Student Grade Retention in Schools." Doctoral dissertation, The University of Wisconsin-Milwaukee. *Dissertation Abstracts International*, 69, 59–60.

Rethinking School Design for Better Learning Outcomes

- The need for redesign: A look at the goals of a redesigned educational system, including assessments.
- Models and methodologies to consider for school and classroom structure: The benefits of multiage classrooms.
- Recommendations for multiage classroom development: Overcoming barriers to multiage classroom implementation.
- Alternative assessments in redesigned schools: A look at more effective models for assessments.

The idea of rethinking the design of American schools is far from new. It has long been recognized that teaching strategies require organizational change so that students and teachers have more contact. Such a change is necessary if high standards are to be maintained while teaching procedures shift. In high-achieving countries, where academic failure is rare, teachers often stay with students for multiple years and teach them multiple subjects. The strategy of having students work with a single teacher or a small group of teachers over a period of several years and for multiple subjects has proven effective in supporting high-level educational goals.

In this chapter, we will outline some of the most viable strategies for redesigning America's public-school systems. Significantly, all of these designs reflect the belief that graded schooling does not support the highest levels of educational achievement.

The Need for Redesign

The American educational system needs to be redesigned; that much is clear. But what should these redesigned goals be? The original goals of public education in the United States concentrated on developing productive and engaged citizens with well-rounded knowledge in a number of key subject areas. It was thought that such citizens would be capable of applying knowledge and skills to function within society and could become providers. The American education system also had a goal of producing citizens who understood the workings of a democratic government and were prepared to participate in the governing of the nation. It was assumed that students should be familiar with the basics of reading, writing, the sciences, mathematics, literature, art, history, and politics.

The purpose, in other words, was set beyond the basis of attaining employment upon graduation from high school. It was about having foundational knowledge and the ability to apply that knowledge, to analyze and infer, but also to appreciate new ideas and concepts, and to be able to work with them.

It is far easier to help a mind perform a single function than to work on developing a mind that can easily adapt and learn to perform many different functions. The current graded education system has the goal of producing graduates who can, after many years of conditioning, regurgitate information under high-stress situations. Essentially, our graduates learn to follow rules or instructions passed on to them.

We can see this in the design of standardized testing. Multiple-choice questions, which so many standardized tests use, do not allow for independent expression of ideas. Indeed, many students with a natural capacity for higher thinking can find themselves struggling with standardized testing simply because they are accustomed to thinking at a higher level. In their analytical thought process, some of the more advanced students go beyond the "simple" answer to a test question.

To redesign the current public-education system, we must go beyond establishing what the current goals of education are and what they have been or might be. We need to also specify why one set of goals—goals targeting higher thinking, independent thought, creativity, and analytics—are more valuable than the present goals that concentrate on a more rigid thought process.

Perhaps the best argument in favor of the former is the future direction of the American and global jobs market. It is widely accepted that knowledge and innovation are the keys to the success of future business ventures. In the past, the most valuable commodities of businesses were physical objects; however, with the emergence of the internet and wireless connectivity, knowledge assets are becoming more important.

Today, knowledge is a primary currency and the ability to apply knowledge is extremely valuable. If, as many reports suggest, knowledge is the currency of the twenty-first century, then the cultivation of this knowledge should be central to our national efforts, including the efforts of our education system (Powell and Snellman 2004).

Investment in innovation often crops up in political conversations. Obama has several times mentioned policies targeting overseas innovators and scientists, and the need to attract such individuals to replenish the knowledge banks of the United States. While there may be many benefits to such a policy, outsourcing innovation in this way is little more than a stopgap measure and does not come close to solving the underlying problem, which lies in our educational institutions.

The knowledge economy is defined as a system for producing and offering services centered on knowledge-intensive activities. It is also a system that inevitably promotes an accelerated rate of technical and scientific development. Associated with this is the rapid obsolescence found in the knowledge economy, in which one idea or product is quickly replaced by another.

Instead of relying on knowledge and the intellectual product of other countries, the United States needs to begin harvesting its own knowledge, its own intellectual product, in the form of well-educated, innovative individuals. The first step in achieving this harvest is an outright revision of the public-education system, at all levels.

The American system needs to revert to its roots and consider the purpose for which public education was initially established in this country and the model provided to us by other nations around the world of what knowledge-focused and innovation-focused education can be, what models work to drive knowledge and innovation, and what models serve to support the needs and talents of those who may not thrive in the typical educational setting.

Models and Methodologies to Consider for School and Classroom Structure

In a classroom with furniture loosely arranged around the teacher's desk, and nooks here and there for reading or pursuing special projects, second-grader Michael is sitting with his teacher, reading a story he wrote about a watermelon. The teacher is enthusiastic, praising Michael and asking him whether he would like to show the story to some of his classmates. He agrees to do so, and they walk over to three third-grade girls who are sitting together at a table working on their own stories. The teacher asks the third-graders whether they would like to listen to Michael's story, and they nod (Goularte 1998).

With plenty of confidence, Michael reads his story aloud, and the third-grade girls listen intently. One of the girls, Vanessa, comments on his choice of vocabulary: she liked his use of the adjective "juicy," she says. They ask him to read the story again, and on the second pass, another girl, Karen, seems perplexed. The teacher asks if she has an issue with the story, and Karen says that she doesn't understand the last line, which reads: "I like watermelon because when you make it." She says that the sentence seems incomplete (Goularte 1998).

Michael is confused. He doesn't know what Karen means when she talks about an incomplete sentence and looks to the teacher for help. The teacher encourages the girls to offer ideas. Vanessa thinks for a moment, and then looks at Michael. "You can say: 'When you make it, it tastes good,'" she offers. Michael thanks her for the suggestion, and he and the teacher return to their original spot. Michael decides he likes Vanessa's proposed revision and changes the end of his story (Goularte 1998).

Multiage classrooms such as the one depicted above are a growing phenomenon in the United States. The process of managing the organization of classrooms by grade is challenging. In a classroom such as Michael's, those challenges are magnified. Yet, if multiage classrooms are a starting point for reorganizing the American public-education system, there are existing models to choose from and the benefits of these models are quite clear.

The multiage classroom described by Leeds and others (Leeds and Marshak 2002) operates according to the following principles: First, students are included in the classroom for at least a two-year span in chronological age. Second, each student in the classroom remains with the same teacher or teachers for at least two years, and often longer.

With this model in place, teachers reported being able to perceive each student not as a member of a graded grouping but as an individual with multiple qualities and capabilities. There is no need to assess each child based solely on his or her level of development, with the graded standards and age-based expectations applied in that assessment context.

One report, for instance, outlines the specific academic, social, and emotional benefits for students, as well as the various benefits for teachers in that environment (Gajadharsingh 1991). The academic benefits included peer tutoring, which involves having older students work directly with younger students to transfer skills and knowledge. Benefits to both the older and younger students, the tutor and the tutee, include more independence and greater confidence. In fact, peer tutoring, as a practice in the classroom, not only builds confidence in children but can help resolve the learning challenges of students who struggle academically. Problem-solving skills can also be easily developed through this approach. Another benefit is that there is more time spent teaching and actually bonding with a struggling child.

Teachers report that they can, in fact, work with failing students. They are most effectively able to do so, they report, during elementary-school years when the problem of retention or promotion is removed. They can also target underlying academic challenges and take the necessary time and steps to address them. The need to judge whether a student is ready to progress to the next grade is no longer relevant. Teachers can look instead at problem-solving through their teaching strategies and use of supplemental supports.

The social and emotional benefits of multiage classrooms must also be considered, especially for students who are struggling academically. Teachers have reported that the multiage classroom model allows for a much greater degree of familiarity and mutual understanding between teacher and students. Deeper relationships can form between teachers and parents, not only because the relationship period is extended, but also because of the enhanced social environment of the classroom (Leeds and Marshak 2002). Because there is greater consistency of teaching expectations and behaviors, there can also be a greater sense of comfort and security within the multiage classroom. This allows those students who might otherwise struggle with transitions to develop a sense of confidence and, in the long term, to concentrate on their academic development, as opposed to worrying about the social component of the classroom experience.

Based on the available research, and in light of the current issues with the graded system, the multiage approach appears to be the best option for redesigning the organization of classrooms. Even so, we would be well advised to consider alternative organizational strategies that make use of age. Multiage classrooms appear to work particularly well for elementary-school-age students, giving younger children time to familiarize themselves with the classroom environment and the learning experience. At the same time, there is a need to recognize that all students are different, and some of these differences in interest, ability, and aptitude are clearly associated with age.

By the time a student enters high school, the educational system should begin to acknowledge that students are approaching the point of entering higher education or the job market. This emphasis is needed to reinforce the student's awareness that the purpose of schooling is to produce educated, moral, and dedicated citizens.

With this in mind, grouping students into educational units based on common ability level would support the needs of the individual at all levels of accomplishment. The goal of each tiered classroom would not be simply to teach the student or the class at some prescribed level. Rather, the goal would be to find each student's areas of weakness and strength, so that teaching methods could be adjusted to challenge as well as support.

Recommendations for Multiage Classroom Development

Paula Carter teaches in a multiage classroom at Rita Cannan Elementary School in Reno, Nevada. Many of the students' parents are involved in the low-income unskilled jobs associated with the gambling industry. Seventy percent speak a language other than English at home and 88 percent qualify for free or reduced-price school lunches. Because of the nature of the work in the city, the transience rate is close to 50 percent. In order to counter this, Rita Cannan Elementary requests that parents keep their children in the school for at least three consecutive years (Carter 2005).

Carter's classroom incorporates first-, second-, and third-grade students. When asked why the school does this, she responds, "I can't think of a good reason not to," and goes on to say that "multiage grouping builds strong relationships among teachers, students, and families." Carter had experienced a model multiage classroom in her university training at the University of Nevada, Reno, and always knew it was something she wanted to try (Carter 2005).

"Older students bring new students into the fold by showing them how the classroom works," she says. "We hear them coaching the younger children: 'Try it again! Don't forget to use your strategies. Get your mouth ready to say the word.'" (Carter 2005).

One ingredient that makes Carter's classroom a success is the fact that she team teaches with Theresa Crowley, who speaks fluent Spanish. This not only facilitates communication with the students; it also helps the parents, many of whom speak no English at all. Initially, Carter and Crowley spent much of their time in planning. However, as their relationship has grown, it has changed and deepened. Carter says, "Now we see ourselves as observers of children, looking at what has transpired in the classroom and what needs to occur to support each student every day" (Carter 2005).

Some outsiders question whether it is possible to implement a multiage classroom. Students from first grade, they say, will have different abilities than students in third grade. However, Carter notes that student abilities differ widely even within a single grade. In her classroom, they group students for various tasks and various purposes, noting that she wants the students to feel as though they are a part of a family. The multiage classroom, in her estimation, works. Recently, she was able to compare students who had spent two years in her classroom with their peers in a single-age classroom. The students in her classroom were more fluent readers, justifying her approach (Carter 2005).

The first and perhaps most obvious barrier to any change in the American public-education system is the parent population. According to some researchers, parents are particularly prone to dissatisfaction and rejection of new models for the education system. They often have concerns for the long-term stability and academic success of their children, and rightly so. Schools should not be an environment in which there is considerable experimentation with standards and procedures. Yes, teachers and administrators—and even students—should be prepared to experiment a bit to understand what models and approaches work best in a specific situation, but even this level of experimentation is expected to occur within the boundaries of academic standards. The last thing most parents want is to have their child participate in an experimental change in education standards, only to find the experiment a failure.

Many parents are not fully aware of the philosophies of multiage classrooms or of the wealth of research supporting them. Many parents have concerns about their children being grouped with other children of different ages and are often worried about the quality of instruction. Such concerns are not unreasonable (Song, Spradlin, and Plucker 2009).

Research has demonstrated that parents who are more involved in school life are usually the ones who prefer to have their children in multiage classrooms. At the same time, the involvement of parents can produce multiage classrooms that are full of privileged and wealthy students, with the possibility that the group becomes less diverse, and thus not in keeping with a philosophy of multiage education programs (Song, Spradlin, and Plucker 2009).

Important considerations include teacher buy-ins, according to Song, Spradlin, and Plucker (2009). Teacher preparedness is another important point that must be addressed in the plans for placing multiage classrooms in settings where they are new. Many teachers featured in reports on multiage classrooms say they received little preparation for teaching students of different ages.

Winning teachers over to the educational philosophy of multiage classrooms is another necessary step for successful implementation. According to one study, eight in ten teachers oppose differentiated instruction (Song, Spradlin, and Plucker 2009). Again, though, adaption of the curriculum to meet the needs of all students in this type of context is difficult. They doubt their own abilities and are unsure of the supports at their disposal to assign groups with different work and to teach the material. Efficiently creating group work among students of different abilities and ages is another area where teachers find themselves struggling. Increased workload is also an issue (Song, Spradlin, and Plucker 2009).

Since teachers with more extensive training and professional development tend to have the opportunity to teach multiage classes, the experience gap between those who teach single-graded classes and those who teach multiage classes can become a problem. That gap is identified as potentially leading to feelings of superiority in multiage groups. Teachers who are opposed to change can undermine well-meaning multiage classroom teachers (Song, Spradlin, and Plucker 2009).

Administrators can also struggle with the concept and management of multiage classrooms. However, their issues are largely due to the federal and state accountability laws that require students to take standardized tests by grade level, as already outlined (Song, Spradlin, and Plucker 2009).

Because multiage classrooms tend to blur the grade-level standards, it can be difficult to fairly administer standardized tests. Furthermore, many principals have reported that it can be difficult to operate two types of structures in one school (Song, Spradlin, and Plucker 2009). Principals have reported that it is challenging because multiage groups often need special field trips, school schedules, and equipment. Occasionally there will be a need for two separate groups for a given event. All of these considerations create challenges for the school administration and budget management. The takeaway is that multiage programs do not fit neatly into the traditional organization for schools; nor are they designed to. However, if our focus is on what is right for the children, rather than what fits neatly into the boxes we've already created, we should be willing to adapt current structures to multiage systems.

According to the research, certain student demographics reap the greatest benefits from multiage classrooms. The demographic that benefits most is one that has both disadvantaged students and high-ability students. In other words, the multi-ability element, which we looked at in chapter six, is important in the multiage classroom, too (Carter 2005).

Of course, this creates a further problem. There are specific challenges to establishing and managing multiage programs in high-poverty schools. It is difficult to organize classes to include a sufficiently diverse group of students in terms of ability. Careful planning can lead to success, however (Carter 2005). In particular, a clear benefit of multiage classrooms is that struggling students can benefit from the resultant learning environment; an environment that is typically caring and supportive of diverse learning. High-ability students also benefit because of the resultant variety and because opportunities are not limited to students who struggle academically. While the various programs for high achievers exist in a variety of forms, some of the examples mentioned in the research include afterschool activities, summer camps, and honor classes—being involved in a diverse population of various ages is also important. Multiage classrooms require the considered development of differentiated curricula and instructions. They require the development of a curriculum that is specifically designed to meet the needs of all students (Lloyd 1999).

High-quality research must be done to assess not only the effects of multiage education in a modern context, essentially updating the research that has already been done, but also to validate, through research and randomized control trials, the optimal procedures and policies for multiage education. Research is also needed to determine exactly what type of curriculum would best serve the multiage classroom environment, as well as how accountability in terms of academic standards and curriculum might be defined and implemented.

Teachers must be educated and prepared to manage multiage classrooms and given intensive support to maintain an appropriate level of professional development over time. It is not enough to promise that there will be support available; the support must be in place and made use of effectively. Honesty and accountability are key factors.

As in any other educational environment, students may not enjoy optimal benefits from multiage classrooms if teachers cannot implement best practices. In this instance, students may not enjoy the benefits of the educational model if teachers don't have the ability to put differentiated instructional strategies, environments, and assessments in place. Offering professional-development workshops on multiage education and supporting differentiated instruction for teachers, as well as providing detailed information for parents, can help students implement multiage programs successfully.

Multiage classrooms are often not aligned with graded and curriculum-centered educational agendas in the United States, and this contributes to the challenges of making the necessary shift. Alignment of the multiage program with curriculum must be emphasized at all points of contact. One of the greatest difficulties for administrators looking to implement the multiage program in traditionally organized schools is that they have to operate two different programs in one school, or have to operate a program that is incompatible with the legal state and federal requirements of accountability.

Whereas school administrators have gone about creating space for multiage classrooms in the past, trying to force them into what already exists, administrators must instead be supported in creating multiage classrooms that exist outside the graded system. School administrators must do more than apply multiage education as a quick-fix solution for the underserved or for those who are not succeeding in the traditional classroom. Multiage classrooms should not be used as a dumping ground, but should be considered, as part of an established multiage program, to be something more substantial. Indeed, administrators must essentially revise their thinking to ensure that multiage classrooms are seen as the best option for providing students with an excellent education. To make multiage classrooms beneficial to all students, administrators should envision the classrooms as a "school within a school" (Stone 2004).

Finally, there is the problem of federal and state accountability and how the existing systems of accountability depend on standards, assessments, and school performance accountability. Creating a K-12 education system that emphasizes the achievement of all students and the academic, social, and emotional development of students is crucial, but it cannot be rushed.

The accountability issues currently manifest as supports for a system that emphasizes the achievement of the "bubble kids," or students just below the passing rates or cut scores on standardized testing (Song, Spradlin, and Plucker 2009). Of course, there should be an emphasis on students who are at the outside of the distribution of abilities, whereas the current emphasis is at the expense of students within these bounds. The lowest achievers and highest-ability students don't have a place with the current model, and creativity and innovation, of course, are lost in the drive to have students demonstrate a level of minimum competency.

Shifting to multiage classrooms should also concentrate on this notion of providing individual students with access to challenging but developmentally appropriate instruction. More than this, though, there should be a clear effort to embrace the potential for creative and innovative learning. The opportunities for this learning and the obvious need for it should be emphasized as one of the principal reasons for the shift to multiage classrooms. The need to embrace the true principles of education is central to all the benefits, challenges, and subsequent recommendations for multiage classroom development and management.

Alternative Assessments in Redesigned Schools

Redesigned schools would require different models for assessment as well. We have already outlined some of the available options, and this section will discuss some of the ways in which those models and strategies might be integrated into a school system that is designed to be multiage and multi-ability.

One of the key benefits of the multiage classroom, and one of the reasons for placing it at the foundation of the design structure for a new school, is that it reduces the need to assess students for the purpose of determining whether they should be promoted or retained. Although assessments do not need to be linked to retention or promotion policies, they do fulfill important functions within the education system. Not least, they let teachers know whether students understand what they are being taught. They also assess the students' ability to apply the skills they are being taught.

Particularly in the elementary-school setting, assessments need to be as nonintrusive as possible to the everyday experience of the students and teachers. Assessments should target students who need additional support, and those who are not doing well academically after the universal interventions should receive first-tier intervention. Assessments also need to identify those students who are excelling and could benefit from additional support aimed at helping gifted students. For students who are meeting expectations and falling within that vast group of typical students, assessments are also important for communicating with parents, reinforcing a positive learning experience for children and helping to amass data that future educators can use to tailor their teaching to specific individuals with their own history of strengths and weaknesses.

In high school, there is a need for some mode of standardized assessment or preparation for standardized assessments. Universities and colleges need to be able to measure student abilities so they know whether an individual is ready for entry to a particular higher-education course. In this environment, standardized tests are entirely appropriate and needed. They should not, however, be the only (or even the primary) form of assessment.

Students should, first of all, benefit from assessments. They should be able to gauge their own progress and be able to show that they can make progress without factors such as the ability to understand the content of the test or test-related stress having an impact upon their evaluation. At the same time, high school assessments should be preparing students for college and employment. The ability to manage stress, work under pressure, and complete tasks within a time limit is important in the workplace (but less important in an educational environment).

One of the better uses of assessment is the assignment of students to particular tiers or academic groupings. For instance, a student who is in the second set for science or modern languages, scoring well on a series of assessments and receiving positive teacher reports, could be rewarded with promotion to the first set and thus to an opportunity to learn at a higher level. Alternatively, a student who did not score well on the second set could be allowed to go to the third set for additional support, to tackle areas of weakness or knowledge gaps that might have emerged. The retention or promotion issue would not have the same negative connotations, though, and there would be the incentive for students, if they were concerned about their current achievement level, to improve their performance and work their way back up to a higher set. To make the system successful, however, appropriate assessment methods must be coupled to appropriate teaching methods and supports.

Overall, assessments should target analytical thought processes, the quality of written expression, the demonstration of understanding, and flexibility of thinking. Rigid, multiple-choice testing should not be used for student assessment. To take advantage of the multiage scenario and the potential for collaboration and peer tutoring, assessments conducted in the form of group projects are a better option.

Duffy's report describes the need for student progress to be carefully monitored over time, using measurements that are tied to local curricular and state content and achievement standards (Duffy 2007). The assessments, however, need to be sensitive enough to pick up the benchmarks that will lead to mastery of specific content. Moreover, there is an obvious need to do away with current local and state-level curricula, and to provide a less rigid model for assessing students based on assumptions related to developmental stage. Even within a multiage classroom, students should demonstrate certain knowledge and skills by age. That demonstration, however, could be relatively flexible, and the mastery of content and skill should be assessed from several different angles and with the recognition that different students mature at different rates. While one student may be able to master certain knowledge and skills earlier than expected, another might require an additional year or more to get to the required level.

Concluding Thoughts

The redesign of America's schools, as this chapter suggests, would involve many levels of change and would take time. Nonetheless, there is immense potential and opportunity to learn about the aspects of the American education system that have been successful in the past and those elements that continue to be successful today. There is also the opportunity to learn from alternative education and assessment models, such as those found in Finland and other European countries. The multiage classroom approach has a great deal to offer the American public as a learning environment that reduces many of the negative elements of the current system—elements that make students anxious about school and uninspired by the process of learning.

The ultimate goal of a redesigned system is the revival of learning as a passion within this nation. One of the qualities the Founding Fathers cherished was curiosity and a love for intellectual development and study. The talent that existed among those who founded this nation is something that should, even today, help rekindle the nation's passion to learn, innovate, and create. This is becoming ever more crucial because of the importance of knowledge and innovation in our global economy.

Inspiring students to be creative, analytical, and resourceful in their thinking will likely have many other effects. The cost of maintaining the status quo includes high unemployment rates and reliance upon public benefits, high school dropout rates that are disproportionately high, and many social and emotional issues that manifest as problems of self-esteem. Creating a passion and a true capacity for learning would help to teach America's students to work for themselves, boosting self-esteem.

It is a feature of our time that new ideas and new technologies are making old systems redundant. This can either be a depressing reality for the American worker, or an inspiring and challenging one. It seems reasonable to assume that the quality of one's education might well tip the balance of perception. An individual who has enjoyed a high-quality, inspiring education that teaches critical thinking and a true appreciation of knowledge in its various forms will be able to apply innovation and creative thinking to new situations. This is the type of American who overcomes challenges instead of being left out in the cold by change.

The innovators of the future will be those who can take existing products and transform them to achieve new results, to perform different or enhanced functions. Ultimately, the American educational system should be focused on making such innovations possible for American minds. Even within the educational system itself, we should be striving to do more with the resources that are available to us, supporting greater efficiency, greater results, and a higher purpose.

References

Carter, P. 2005. "The Modern Multi-Age Classroom." *The Whole Child*, 63(1), 54–58.

Duffy, H. 2007. *Meeting the Needs of Significantly Struggling Learners in High School: A Look at Approaches to Tiered Intervention*. American Institutes for Research. Retrieved from http://files.eric.ed.gov/fulltext/ED501084.pdf.

Gajadharsingh, J. 1991. "CEA Research Study on the Multi-grade Classroom." In *The Multi-Grade Classroom: Myth and Reality: A Canadian Study*, 57–81. Edited by Margaret Gayfer. Toronto, Ontario: Canadian Education Association.

Goularte, R. 1998. "Components of a Successful Multiage Classroom." *Share2 Learn*. Accessed September 12, 2016. http://www.share2learn.com/components.html.

Leeds, A., and D. Marshak. 2002. *The Benefits of the Multiage Classroom: Teaching and Learning in the Intermediate Classroom*. Lanham, MD: Scarecrow Press.

Lloyd, L. 1999. "Multi-Age Classes and High Ability Students." *Review of Educational Research*, 69(2), 187–212. Accessed September 12, 2016. http://eric.ed.gov/ERICWebPortal/custom/portlets/recordDetails/detailmini.jsp?_nfpb=true&_&ERICExtSearch_SearchValue_0=EJ600456&ERICExtSearch_SearchTy pe_0=no&accno=EJ600456.

Powell, W. W., and K. Snellman. 2004. "The Knowledge Economy." *Annual Review of Sociology*, 30, 199–220. Accessed September 12, 2016. http://www.stanford.edu/group/song/papers/powell_snellman.pdf.

Song, R., T. E. Spradlin, and J. A. Plucker. 2009. "Advantages and Disadvantages of Multiage Classrooms in the Era of the NCLB Accountability." *Education Policy Brief*, 7(1), Winter, 1–8.

Stone, Sandra. 2004. *Creating the Multiage Classroom*. Glenview, IL: Good Year Books.

Taylor & Francis eBooks

Helping you to choose the right eBooks for your Library

Add Routledge titles to your library's digital collection today. Taylor and Francis ebooks contains over 50,000 titles in the Humanities, Social Sciences, Behavioural Sciences, Built Environment and Law.

Choose from a range of subject packages or create your own!

Benefits for you
- Free MARC records
- COUNTER-compliant usage statistics
- Flexible purchase and pricing options
- All titles DRM-free.

Benefits for your user
- Off-site, anytime access via Athens or referring URL
- Print or copy pages or chapters
- Full content search
- Bookmark, highlight and annotate text
- Access to thousands of pages of quality research at the click of a button.

Free Trials Available
We offer free trials to qualifying academic, corporate and government customers.

eCollections – Choose from over 30 subject eCollections, including:

Archaeology	Language Learning
Architecture	Law
Asian Studies	Literature
Business & Management	Media & Communication
Classical Studies	Middle East Studies
Construction	Music
Creative & Media Arts	Philosophy
Criminology & Criminal Justice	Planning
Economics	Politics
Education	Psychology & Mental Health
Energy	Religion
Engineering	Security
English Language & Linguistics	Social Work
Environment & Sustainability	Sociology
Geography	Sport
Health Studies	Theatre & Performance
History	Tourism, Hospitality & Events

For more information, pricing enquiries or to order a free trial, please contact your local sales team:
www.tandfebooks.com/page/sales

 **Routledge** — The home of Routledge books

www.tandfebooks.com

For Product Safety Concerns and Information please contact our EU representative GPSR@taylorandfrancis.com
Taylor & Francis Verlag GmbH, Kaufingerstraße 24, 80331 München, Germany

www.ingramcontent.com/pod-product-compliance
Lightning Source LLC
Chambersburg PA
CBHW061842300426
44115CB00013B/2479